University of Birmingham

URBAN AND REGIONAL STUDIES NO 6

III Planning for Change

University of Birmingham

URBAN AND REGIONAL STUDIES

No 1.   Recreation Research and Planning
edited by Thomas L. Burton

No 2.   Experiments in Recreation Research
by Thomas L. Burton

No 3.   The Urban Future
by John N. Jackson

No 4.   The Social Framework of Planning
by J. B. Cullingworth

No 5.   The Social Content of Planning
by J. B. Cullingworth

Also by J. B. Cullingworth

Town and Country Planning in Britain

Housing and Local Government

Problems of an Urban Society

VOLUME III
Planning for Change

Edited by J. B. CULLINGWORTH

LONDON · GEORGE ALLEN & UNWIN LTD
Ruskin House   Museum Street

Made and printed in Great Britain
in 10 point Times New Roman
by William Clowes & Sons, Limited
London, Beccles and Colchester

Contents

The Contributors

Melvin M. Webber: Director, Institute of Urban and Regional Development, University of California, Berkeley

William Alonso: Professor of Regional Planning at the University of California, Berkeley

David Donnison et al: Director and staff members of the Centre for Environmental Studies, London

Peter Levin: Lecturer in Social Administration, London School of Economics

Peter Willmott: Director of the Institute of Community Studies, London

Adrian Sinfield: Senior Lecturer in Sociology, University of Essex

J. Michael Thomson: Rees Jeffreys Research Fellow at the London School of Economics

J. B. Cullingworth: Director of the Planning Exchange (West Central Scotland), Glasgow; Formerly Professor and Director of the Centre for Urban and Regional Studies, University of Birmingham

Acknowledgements

Grateful acknowledgement is made to authors and publishers for permission to reproduce these papers:

Melvin M. Webber: 'Planning in an Environment of Change', *Town Planning Review*, Volume 39, No. 3 & 4, October 1968 and January 1969, pp. 179–195 and 277–295. Reprinted by permission of the Bartlett Society and the editor of the *Town Planning Review*.

W. Alonso: 'Beyond the Inter-disciplinary Approach to Planning', *Journal of the American Institute of Planners*, Volume 37, No. 3, May 1971, pp. 169–173. Reprinted by permission of the *Journal of the American Institute of Planners*.

Centre for Environmental Studies: *Observations on the Greater London Development Plan* (November 1970). Reprinted by permission of the Centre for Environmental Studies.

P. Levin and D. V. Donnison: 'People and Planning', *Public Administration*, Vol. 49, Winter 1969, pp. 473–479. Reprinted by permission of the editor of *Public Administration*.

P. Willmott: 'Some Social Trends', *Urban Studies*, Volume 6, No. 3, November 1969, pp. 286–308. Reprinted by permission of the editor of *Urban Studies*.

Crowther Report: 'Population Changes and their Educational Consequences' (pp. 28–35 of *15 to 18*, HMSO, 1959). Reprinted by permission of the Controller of Her Majesty's Stationery Office.

A. Sinfield: 'Poverty Rediscovered', *Race*, Volume X, No. 3, October 1968, pp. 202–9 (with additional note and updated bibliography). Reprinted by permission of the Institute of Race Relations.

J. M. Thomson: 'Half-way to a Motorized Society', *Lloyds Bank Review*, October 1971, pp. 16–34. Reprinted by permission of the editor of *Lloyds Bank Review*.

Department of the Environment: *Long-Term Population Distribution in Great Britain*, HMSO, 1971, Chapter 7 (pages 89–95). Reprinted by permission of the Controller of Her Majesty's Stationery Office.

Summary of Contents of Volumes I and II

Introduction

Few areas of debate have burgeoned in recent years as much as those concerned with urban problems. The reasons stem only in part from the growth of problems of urban decay, pollution, poverty, regional decline and the like. Of equal, if not greater importance are changing attitudes, changes in public awareness and in the limits of public toleration. As the complexities and interdependencies of modern life have increased, so has the resolve to combat the environmental and social ills to which these give rise. Concern for the quality of the environment is no longer the preserve of an intellectual minority of visionaries, administrators and politicians: it is a matter of concern to an electorate which is demanding greater 'citizen-participation' and more effective control over the vast and amorphous managerial institutions of contemporary society. At the same time the threshold of tolerability has changed. The number of the homeless and the destitute is certainly less now than it was a century or even a generation ago, but it is not the statistics which are currently 'shocking'; it is the fact that homelessness and destitution exist at all which has become intolerable. Of course, 'standards' have risen and concepts of poverty have changed beyond the wildest dreams of nineteenth-century reformers. But this is irrelevant: each generation has to define for itself the criteria against which poverty is to be judged. Similarly with the physical environment. That towns are now relatively healthy places in which to live is a statistical fact, but this is of little relevance in the context of contemporary concern for the quality of the urban environment.

The point should not, however, be overstressed. The festering sores of slumdom still exist in some major cities and these bear a tragic resemblance to those described at length in the blue books of the nineteenth century. Further, they are hidden from—or, at least, are unseen by—the middle class commuter and, therefore, do not shock the public conscience or precipitate the necessary public action. There are no longer cholera epidemics to overcome ignorance of the conditions that exist. At the same time individualistic moral philosophy has been given a modern twist with the perceived (yet unrealized) advent of 'the welfare state' and the defensive mechanisms

15

rapidly and eloquently brought into play by the institutions of social welfare whenever major criticisms are made of their adequacy by social commentators. Curiously—and dangerously—the criticism of public and social service has become institutionalized to such an extent that 'direct action' is increasingly seen by some as being the only route to a change in 'the system'. At present the balance is heavily in favour of legitimized change within the system: by reform of institutional procedures, by consultative councils, by ombudsmen and, less surely, by neighbourhood groups. New styles of local government and new divisions of power are under serious discussion. Though there is a clear trend towards agreement on the need for large local authorities able to command substantial resources, responsible for meaningful areas of community interest, and capable of accepting a substantial devolution of power from central government, there is also a widely accepted need for truly local institutions able to express neighbourhood feelings and to undertake direct responsibility for matters which are of only local concern. The main debate, however, is surefooted only in the former field where the issues are clear (though difficult to evaluate and balance one against the other): so far as 'community councils' (to use the term employed in the new legislation on Local Government) are concerned, the debate has barely progressed beyond recognition of the need.

Reference is made throughout these three volumes to these and similar issues relating to the distribution of power, and an attempt is made, in the last chapter of Volume II, to draw the threads together, but the main purpose is less ambitious; it is to provide an outline of some of the major urban problems of contemporary Britain. The qualifying 'some' is essential, both because of the competence of the author to discuss all the relevant issues and also because the field is limitless. The majority of the population live in urban areas. What then should be the criterion by which some issues are included as 'urban and regional problems', while others are excluded? There is no easy answer to this and no claim is made that this book demonstrates one. The 'solution' is personal but, hopefully, not idiosyncratic. The intention has been to provide an introduction to those issues which, on one view, are among the more important.

The three volumes complement *Town and Country Planning in Britain* which gives an outline of the apparatus of physical planning, but their focus is on problems and on social and (to a lesser extent) economic aspects. Some degree of overlap between the two works has been inevitable while, on the other hand, attempts to avoid this have led to a rather more slender treatment of some issues (such as 'amenity') than might have been expected.

A common thread throughout is the inter-connectedness of issues. This presents a perpetual—and probably insoluble—problem for government, which must divide its responsibilities into manageable parts. A similar problem faces an author who attempts to provide a broad picture of the issues, even when the field is narrower and, within that field, comprehensiveness is explicitly disclaimed. To illustrate: should the transport problems of elderly people be dealt with in a discussion of transport or in a discussion of the elderly? Should issues relating to the size and composition of the labour force come under the heading of 'demography' or 'economics'? Is it more appropriate to deal with housing subsidies in the context of housing or that of poverty?

In practice the solution adopted matters less than the awareness that there are always different, and possibly equally relevant, contexts for each aspect of a many-sided issue. What is totally inadequate is to approach a 'problem' in the terms of a discipline or a profession. Economics, sociology and, indeed, all the separate social sciences are abstractions which deal with parts of problems defined by the nature of their analytical tools. In a similar way, professions deal with parts of problems defined by the nature of their corpus of knowledge and their operational skills; and government departments and ministers deal with parts of problems defined by the nature of the responsibilities which have been allocated to them.

The development of multi-disciplinary studies, of generic professions and of non-departmental offices are all attempts to break down these artificial barriers. These three volumes are offered as a modest contribution to the same endeavour.

The intention in dividing this work into three volumes was simple and logical. Volume I would set the framework within which specific problems could be discussed in Volume II. Volume III would then provide a set of complementary readings. As with all good plans, implementation proved less simple. The subject matter refused to be so neatly packaged. Where does the 'framework' end and the 'problem' begin? By the time the plan had been finalized it no longer seemed to have the validity which it had at conception. Nevertheless, the underlying concept of a three volume series spanning major contemporary urban problems remained.

Volume I: The Social Framework of Planning

In the first volume there is a general discussion of the demographic, socio-economic and physical framework of 'planning', together with an account of the problems of urban traffic and a note on the land values problem.

17

The starting point is the size and structure of the population, recent demographic trends and their implications. This is prefaced by a short discussion on the concept of an 'optimum' population. The fact that this is elusive and difficult does not detract from its importance. Recognition of this has developed markedly in the twelve months since the first draft was written.

Demographic analysis rapidly becomes indigestible, and no attempt is made to achieve a comprehensive coverage. The aim is to provide sufficient to demonstrate some of the more important implications of current trends. The chapter includes, as a 'case study' some detailed figures on the South East Region: chosen mainly because of the wealth of available material on this Region.

The second chapter, on the socio-economic framework, deals in the main with employment, regional problems and policies and urban growth policy. Again the concept of the 'optimum' is introduced, this time in relation to towns. But while the idea of an optimum population is viewed sympathetically, that of an optimum size of towns is severely criticized particularly in view of the fact that controls over the growth of towns have formed a major plank of British planning policy, frequently with unintended and undesirable effects.

There is, of course, a clash here between a number of different objectives. This is more clearly seen in Chapter 3 which presents an even more selective treatment of the physical framework of planning problems and policies. The selected issues include urban growth, agriculture, forestry, water and natural resources. Since this chapter was drafted an important official study has been published on *Long Term Population Distribution in Great Britain*. An Appendix to Chapter 3 reproduces some of the main findings of this study. (A summary of the Report is reproduced in Volume III.)

Chapter 4 discusses urban traffic problems. This leans heavily (though by no means uncritically) on the writings of Professor Colin Buchanan. Emphasis is laid on environmental issues, road pricing and the development of public transport. Public support for these is currently growing. Unfortunately, no viable system of pricing has yet been devised and policy is therefore constrained to the narrower issue of parking controls.

Finally, a note is provided on the land values problem. This was forced to the fore of public debate just after the appropriate machinery for coping with it (the Land Commission) had been abolished. Though there is some reference to the immediately current problem, the main emphasis of the chapter is on the broader issues. As with the majority of the problems discussed, practicable solutions depend upon public understanding and political leadership. The two schemes introduced by Labour Governments (in 1947 and 1967) failed politically and it is not easy to be hopeful that a third attempt will provide a long-term solution. Nevertheless there are, again, signs of changes in public opinion.

Volume II: The Social Content of Planning

Much of the second volume is concerned with urban poverty and disadvantage: the relative lack of command over resources and access to opportunity and power. Chapter 1 provides a review of the dimensions of poverty and serves as an introduction to the fuller discussion of selected issues in the chapters that follow.

Chapter 2 discusses the nature of housing policies, the special characteristics of housing and a number of issues relating to tenure and choice. The issue of 'choice' emerges more clearly in the chapter on slum clearance and improvement. In both chapters, the differences between the institutional frameworks of 'public' and 'private' housing are underlined. Unfortunately, though justified in historical terms, these differences now create additional 'housing' problems which are further exacerbated by political approaches to 'council housing' and 'owner-occupation'.

Chapter 4, on 'race and colour' is a documentation of the emergence and recognition of a new urban problem which has its roots in human prejudice and fear. Government is here faced with a series of difficult and delicate political problems. The problems are complicated by the fact that they are inextricably intertwined with wider issues of social justice and equality.

The 'colour problem' has resulted in a greater awareness of the social objectives and social implications of physical planning policies. This forms the subject of an extended discussion, in Chapter 5, of the nature and scope of 'social planning'. Increasingly, however, it is being recognized that 'the social' is but a label for one aspect of planning, in the same way that 'the physical' or 'the economic' are labels for other aspects.

Throughout these chapters there is repeated reference to issues such as citizen participation, the distribution of power, and the essentially political nature of all 'planning'. The final chapter attempts a broad review of these issues and stresses the crucial importance of the political process. 'Planning' is essentially, not the fulfilment of plans, but a process of balancing conflicting claims on scarce resources and of achieving compromises between conflicting interests.

19

Volume III: Planning for Change

The third volume is intended not only to complement the first two volumes, but also to bring together a number of important papers on some crucial contemporary urban problems. The major theme is set out at length in Professor Mel Webber's challenging paper which lends its title (in abbreviated form) to the volume as a whole: what are the possibilities, the scope and the content of planning in a rapidly changing society? Some authors are more sure of themselves than others, though most raise more questions than can be answered.

The widespread interest raised by Webber's paper (originally delivered to the Bartlett Society and later printed in the *Town Planning Review*) is a result not only of the cogency of his argument and the felicity of his presentation, but also its particular timeliness. The 1960s saw the increasing rejection of deterministic, detailed 'development' planning and the increasing acceptance of flexible 'structure' planning. The impact was greater on thinking than on practice, but the new thinking underlay the planning legislation which was passed at the end of the decade. Moreover, Webber's 'permissive planning' approach was explicitly adopted in *The Plan for Milton Keynes* (to which Webber personally contributed).

The wider view of 'planning' has led to the creation of inter-disciplinary planning teams. Professor Alonso, in the second paper in this volume, questions the adequacy of these. He sees the inter-disciplinary team primarily as a source of innovation or dissent where new departures are called for. A new approach ('beyond the inter-disciplinary approach') is needed, in which urban and regional problems are dealt with by professionals who are first and foremost specialists in these problems and only secondarily members of traditional disciplines. This 'meta-disciplinary' approach is essentially problem-orientated—a point which arises again in the final paper of this volume.

The paper by Professor Donnison and his colleagues at the Centre for Environmental Studies, though focused on the Greater London Development Plan, demonstrates the inter-connectedness of urban problems and the way difficulties in solving them are exacerbated by definitions of areas of administrative and political responsibility.

This paper was submitted to the Greater London Development Plan Inquiry in November 1970, and has not previously been published.

One of the points raised at the end of this paper is the difficulty facing the public in participating in the debate on the Greater London Development Plan. Yet public participation is now supposedly part

of the planning process. The Skeffington Committee dealt specifically with this issue. Its Report, *People and Planning* is the subject
of further analysis in the fourth paper, by Levin and Donnison. The
Report is shown to be only the beginning of an important debate,
but though a number of proposals are put forward, Levin and
Donnison necessarily conclude with more questions than answers.

With Peter Willmott's paper, modestly entitled 'Some Social
Trends', we return to a theme touched upon in the second chapter
of the first volume: the changing socio-economic framework. This
broad review of social change in Britain argues that strong social
forces are at work leading to a more homogeneous life-style.

A major element in current social change is demographic. Chapter
6 reproduces a short extract from the Crowther Report *15 to 18*
which discusses demographic trends in the context of their educational consequences.

Much of the debate in the sixties was preoccupied with the problems of affluence, but each generation, apparently has to 'rediscover'
poverty. Adrian Sinfield's succinct paper (which extends the discussion contained in Chapter 1 of Volume II) reviews the state of
knowledge on, and the awareness of, poverty in Britain. Originally
published in 1968, its extensive bibliography has been up-dated.

Michael Thomson's paper on traffic provides a survey of the
problems of a society which is about half-way to the 'saturation
level' of around one car to every two people. The title is deliberately
tendentious since it is argued that a fully 'motorized' society is
neither possible nor, indeed, desirable.

The study which is summarized in Chapter 9 exemplifies a broad
approach which has important policy implications. This study, of
Long Term Population Distribution in Great Britain is perhaps the
most important review since the Barlow Report. The fact that the
study was carried out by civil servants (rather than a committee of
inquiry or a Royal Commission) affects the style, but not the mes-
sage. In essence this is that the scope for government intervention,
control and direction is limited. As with Webber the emphasis is on
the need for flexibility. However, there remains a large area for
political debate here, which an expansion of research effort could
render more profitable.

Research is the subject of the final chapter which reproduces,
without amendment, the editor's Inaugural Lecture at the University
of Birmingham. This suffers from its brevity but, following the
publication of, and debate on, the Rothschild and Dainton Reports
(in *A Framework for Government Research and Development*, HMSO,
1971) it has an unexpected topicality. 'Planning for Change', if it is

21

to be relevant and effective, demands a strong research base. But, as the paper argues, research workers must be wary of over-enthusiastic politicians. Research can provide information, understanding and advice, but the responsibility for decision making rests with politicians.

J. B. C.

Chapter 1

Planning in an Environment of Change

MELVIN M. WEBBER

Part I: Beyond the Industrial Age

A NEW CONCEPT OF THE FUTURE

We are constantly amazed at the speed with which our images and attitudes absorb new ideas and new technologies. Novelty appears to have a rapid decay rate in the modern Western world. Once television was made cheap enough for mass distribution, it quickly became part of people's every-day lives. Within a year after Sputnik was launched, space shots scarcely seemed remarkable any more, even though the recent satellites' experiment packages are surely far more sophisticated achievements than the vehicles that orbit them. Then, when satellite transmission of television broadcasts became work-a-day, we readily accepted simultaneous world-wide visual communication as just another clever technological novelty. By next year, heart-transplants will scarcely warrant notice by the news media. And so it has gone, step by step, each dramatic achievement—even the un-anticipated big leap—has a way of becoming commonplace after the fact.

Because we have lacked adequate predictive theory of technological or social change, we have tended to confront each incremental development as it occurs, regarding it as a unitary, independent event. Few people have tried to trace the waves of repercussions that those events might in turn generate through the larger systems of which they become new component parts. Fewer still have tried to predict the chains of consequences that numerous and *cumulative* changes would then induce within the larger systems. And so we have calmly accepted each new accretion, telling ourselves that 'the more things change, the more they remain the same'.

Virtually everyone now knows that the rate of discovery and invention has been explosive during these past two decades; and yet we in the developed world seem to have accepted even that fact as a stable condition and take rapid change as a normal, no-change condition. Perhaps this is a further indication of our large adaptive capacities—in both senses of that phrase: first, that modern social systems have been able to absorb new development without permitting them to rock the social order and, secondly, that we must *believe* that change is no-change, for to believe otherwise would itself upset our perceptions of social order. However, even if true in the past, this is not likely to go on. Knowledge of physical, biological, and social systems is expanding at such a fantastic rate that it is triggering off an equally fantastic expansion in the technologies through which those systems can be modified. These new intellectual resources are making it increasingly possible to anticipate future scientific discovery and technological invention and to forecast some subsequent social effects of discovery and invention. As social theory improves, we are likely to be better able to forecast social change too. In turn, better forecasts will permit us deliberately to plan our responses to those anticipated outcomes—even to select, in some fields, those of the possible outcomes that we happen to prefer. This is to say, in effect, that among the consequences of the knowledge explosion is the emergence of a new way of thinking about the future. That conception is the derivative of our new capacities for prediction, our new images of our powers for controlling future events and, hence, a new outlook suggesting that, to a considerable degree, maybe we really can invent the future.

This new concept of the future represents a remarkable change, a change that is potentially as important as any of the developments that are now building up in the developed world. Let me here simply state my thesis, which I will elaborate upon later.

Pre-industrial societies around the world all seem to be marked by a common perception that the future lies outside the field of vision and certainly outside control. The accumulating studies of peasant and primitive societies are revealing a common fatalism in virtually all of them. Some (the Sioux Indians are one example) do not even have a word for 'future' in their languages. Others that do conceive of future time see its events as in the hands of the gods.

With the coming of industrialization and the commercial economy, possibilities for forward scheduling of production and the requirements for monetary credit provoked a different image of the future. Within the short-run, managers found they could shape the institutions under their control. Observed and anticipated stability in growth rates permitted banks to make loans, with the prospect that they would be repaid. Population forecasters could extrapolate trend lines with some confidence that whatever determined birth and death rates in the immediate past would probably continue to affect them in the immediate future. Indeed, a large insurance industry was in fact built upon the actuarial estimates of probabilities that grew out of these measurements of system stability. For that matter, the whole of the industrial structure was built against the conception of the future that saw a sufficient degree of stability in the short run to justify investment. To account for those future changes that were not or could not be anticipated, the market system developed to feed information on change back into decision centres, so that managers and consumers could then adjust their predictions.

In brief, in the vernacular conception of the industrial age, the future was seen as closely resembling the present; where conditions and events would depart from the present, the response was to *accommodate* to those conditions and events.

The big change which is commented on later, is the current shift away from that image of stability and accommodative response. With the emergence of the post-industrial stage of development, the future is being seen to depart drastically from the present, and it now looks as though men will be seeking more directly to design the future. If we can characterize a single distinguishing difference between the outlooks of the industrial age and of the post-industrial age it is this: that industry and government in the recent past had to respond to change after the fact; in the post-industrial age they will be intellectually equipped to respond before. That is to say, that the coming style for confronting the future will be forecasting and planning.

We are already seeing the signs of this new post-industrial outlook in the rapid rise of new quasi-science of futurism and, in parallel, the rise of a large number of new kinds of planning institutions. These signs are seen in the projective work of such groups as Resources for the Future in Washington, Professor de Jouvenal's Futuribles group on France, The American Academy of Arts and Science's Commission on the Year 2000 and its several committees on the next ten years. In London, there are the Social Science Research Council's project on The Next Thirty Years, and the Centre for Environmental Studies' group on Developing Patterns of Urbanization. There are more. By now there is a literal flood of new institutes on the future being organized in America and elsewhere. Their counterparts are the new planning institutions with such unlikely names as CONSAD Research Corporation, the RAND Corporation, Systems Development Corporation, and the even more unlikely names Lockheed Aircraft Corporation, Aero-Jet General, Litton Industries, and so on.

The best of the new students of the future are trying to foresee latent qualitative consequences before they become manifest—in effect, to develop an early-warning-system that might signal impending disasters, as well as potentially beneficial outcomes that might be exploited were appropriate action be taken soon enough.

Most important, they are attempting to trace out the alternative future histories—particularly the social and economic histories—that would be shaped by plausibly foreseen uncontrollable events and by deliberately designed ones.

Despite the excitement and fashion that is marking this activity, this is probably no fad. Had we been in the forecasting business before, the rise of futurist studies might have been foreseen as a deterministic outcome of the current knowledge explosion. More knowledge, better theory, and improved methods were bound to make conscious confrontation of emphatic and rapid social change inevitable.

Of course, neither students of the future nor practitioners of planning are new phenomena in our midst. There have been individual prophets and forecasters at work for a long time, but these men have typically been aberrants within the world of scholarship. Although scholars generally agree that the test of a theory is its capacity to predict well, theorists in the social and behavioural sciences have traditionally eschewed projective modes of thought in favour of observational modes; and they have done so just as firmly as they have declined normative interpretation in favour of positivistic accounts. The thing that is new is the emergence of a legitimate and organized activity, explicitly devoted to systematic and normative interpretation of potential future histories.

All this can be read as very good news to the city planners, who had for so long been the lonely custodians of a futurist tradition. But this new futurist enterprise can also be read as a serious challenge to the traditional thoughtways and activities of city planning. It is doubtful if city planning will ever be the same again once the impact of this new attitude toward the future, the new predictive technology, and the emerging theoretic sophistication begin to impinge upon it.

City planners have always claimed, of course, that their business is to influence, if not to shape, the future. But until recently, we have been pre-viewing history through very inadequate binoculars. The theory we have had to rely upon has never been good enough. Data have always been too sparse and ill-suited to our wants. Our methods have been too naïve to deal with the complexities of contemporary urbanism. Further, images of the future have always been shaped by the outlook of the industrial age. On all these counts, the new futurism should supply intellectual reinforcements that we have long wished for. This is not to suggest that we shall soon find the magic that will permit us to design the ideal future city. That is neither politically possible nor ethically tolerable. The course of history cannot be controlled either for, as the old-fashioned idea holds, there are logic-

26

ally derivative chains of developmental steps, such that certain social or technological changes determine those that follow.

That deterministic view might seem to be in contradiction with the growing stochastic view that sees events as probabilistic outcomes, and with the older teleologic view that sees history as the resultant of purposive, goal-seeking behaviour of men. These three conceptions are not in contradiction, only in competition.

As planners, we are well served by each. Insofar as our theory and their derivative models can help us to predict deterministically, we can act with greater confidence about the coming changes. Insofar as we can predict probabilistically, we can reduce the odds of error. And, insofar as we can teleologically set out goals and matching actions, we can accomplish the ends we seek. History, however, is not teleologically shaped to the degree that city planners have traditionally presumed. We *can* consciously force some events to happen. But not all. Much of the future will continue to lie outside our control, and we shall have to conform. Some can be approached only with the attitude of the gambler. And some of it can be invented and planned.

Our continuing intellectual problem will be to know when it is most useful to view the future deterministically, when it is best to view it stochastically (and hence as indeterminate), and when we can profitably view it teleologically. That question is likely to take on the character of an intellectual dilemma. In a setting of rapid technological and social change, the possibilities for 'accurate' prediction would seem to decline. But with improving predictive theory, we should also be able more sensitively to anticipate coming changes. And with increasing organizational capacities for large-scale decision and action, we should be able deliberately to shape more of the future than was once possible. No formula is available for resolving these competing views. It may be that the conceptual, methodological and governmental issues that surround these images will continue to occupy us as we are carried along into the coming decades.

SOME SIGNS OF THE FUTURE

Despite the diversity within the community of futurist students, there is a striking consensus among them concerning some of the major historical changes that appear to be under way. Nearly all are by now persuaded that the industrial age is coming to an imminent end in the Western developed nations, and with it the end of the age of the industrial city. For a profession that emerged in response to the industrial city, this forecast must surely be of fundamental interest.

Today, when history is speeding up so rapidly, these commentators

27

agree on one thing if nothing else: that western society is at a major turning point and that future society will differ vastly from contemporary society. In an article in a recent issue of *Encounter*, Professor Brzezinski put it flatly and unambiguously:

> Ours is no longer the conventional revolutionary era; we are entering a novel metamorphic phase in human history. The world is on the eve of a transformation more dramatic in its historic and human consequences than that wrought by the French or the Russian revolutions. Viewed from the long perspective, these famous revolutions merely scratched the surface of the human condition. The changes they precipitated involved alterations in the distribution of power and property within society; they did not affect the essence of individual and social existence. Life—personal and organized—continued much as before, even though some of its external forms (primarily political) were substantially altered. Shocking though it may sound to their acolytes, by the year 2000 it will be accepted that Robespierre and Lenin were mild reformers.[1]

He then goes on to say that 'Unlike the revolutions of the past, the developing metamorphosis will have no charismatic leaders with strident doctrines, but its impact will be more profound' and, it can be added, more subtle. The major current generators of these changes, he notes, include the computers and the new advances in electronic communication, which are fundamentally 'altering the mores, the social structure, and the values of society'. And the work of the futurists, he reports, already 'indicates that men living in the developed world will undergo during the next decades a mutation potentially as basic as that experienced through the slow process of evolution from animal to human status'.

It is not possible to present here a plausible and coherent scenario that might describe the unfolding of the revolutionary era that we will find ourselves in. But some events that already appear to be 'in the cards' can be recounted.

Because the United States is farthest along the paths toward post-industrial status and because most studies of the future are still localized there, the evidence will be drawn mainly from American experience. Insofar as the path beyond the industrial age is deterministic, the American experience is a precursor of future events in other highly developed societies as well.

The most apparent signal of post-industrialism is the shift in the composition of occupations. Industrialization initially moved men out of farming and related extractive industries at a rapid rate. (In the

United States the proportion of the labour force in primary industries fell from around 90 per cent in 1800 to 75 per cent in 1900 to about 5 per cent today, and it is still falling.) In Britain the current proportion is under 4 per cent. How would people have reacted to a forecaster 100 years ago who predicted that only 4 per cent of the labour force could produce all the products of farming, forestry, and fishing?

There was initially a counter-expansion that absorbed the labour force in manufacturing and related jobs—the ratio went from about 5–10 per cent in 1800 to 37 per cent in 1900. It has fluctuated around that level throughout this century, but it is now declining both as a percentage of total employment and in actual number. (In Britain it has varied between 43 per cent and 49 per cent during the 1910–1964 period.) Recently in the United States there has actually been a net loss in numbers of manufacturing jobs during the past ten years, as the service occupations have been expanding. Now, for the first time in the history of the world, there is a nation which employs more people in service than in manufacturing occupations. That in itself is a revolutionary event of dramatic order.

Despite the reduction of manufacturing employment and despite the reduction of the work week (from 60 hours in 1900 to 40 hours today) manufacturing productivity is still growing, repeating the history of agriculture, which reached its most productive stage only when it decanted its labour in favour of machines. The trends in productivity show no signs of abating. Someone at the RAND Corporation recently made the wild guess that America will eventually be able to satisfy all its needs with a mere 2 per cent of its labour force. His guess is a cartoon, of course; but his point is right.

Behind the rise in manufacturing productivity and the move into the service occupations lies the knowledge explosion that continues to impel the changes. Modern manufactured goods are congealed information; they are the products of intensive, organized research-and-development work that employs highly trained minds and sophisticated techniques. The machines that produce the machines are themselves the product of similarly intensive intellectual inputs. The jobs they create require long periods of training, frequently university-based training.

The rising demand for these sorts of R & D workers is being paralleled by a rising demand for other sorts of highly trained specialists—the university teachers, physicians, lawyers, management consultants, and the large varieties of other skilled specialists that complex organization and complex society demand. It is the contributors to and the practitioners within the knowledge industries who are now finding themselves on the crest of the new history.

Indeed, the knowledge industry is fast becoming the new centre of influence and power, with the university and the 'R & D' firm assuming the roles that corporations and labour unions have recently occupied.

A coming repetition of the agricultural and manufacturing revolutions will be hitting the service industries in force before long. One reason people have been able to find jobs in the services is that the productivity of these occupations has so far remained low. But the signs of a change are already clear in banking, book-keeping, and inventory control, where computers have found a ready application; in retail distribution, where customer self-service and mail-order service have reduced the need for sales clerks; and even in machine repair, where it is becoming cheaper to discard worn out parts and to replace them with plug-in components than to repair them. To the degree that cybernation can eventually take over the tedious repetitive service jobs, man-hour productivity will rise and demands for employees will fall.

Some futurists, most notably Donald Michael at the University of Michigan,[2] are confidently predicting that even middle-level white-collar management jobs will be rapidly falling before the competences of cybernation. As a result, the vast office staffs that have been performing these sorts of tasks are already being displaced. Similarly, routine personnel management jobs, engineering staff jobs, quality-control inspection jobs, and others are being better done by computers; and the bigger and faster machines that are now in the works will have far greater capacities than present models. As a result, the routine office-based paper-work occupations may soon go the way of the manual manufacturing occupations.

To be sure, ever since the cybernation revolution hit us in the mid-1950's, some persons have been heralding the time when the work of advanced societies would be largely consigned to machines, and men would be freed for non-work activities. It is true that it has not happened quite as rapidly as some of them had thought, in part because we have not yet found an adequate alternative means for distributing income other than through employment, in part because many of the service wants of advanced societies are very far from being satisfied. There still remain large latent demands for professional and sub-professional aides in the health services, education, child-rearing and, indeed, in the expanding knowledge industries themselves that could absorb unemployed labour for some time to come. Sport and entertainment are presently occupying increasing numbers of performers. As the volume of free spectator-hours increases with the declining work-week and extended vacations, these are likely to become major industries. But the prospect of massive non-employment is, for the first time in history, becoming real. The United States may soon be passing the threshold at which a full employment economy becomes an anachronistic goal.

As Mario Salvadori has put it, in pre-industrial times 'work was . . . a personal human necessity. A man who could not or would not work was the prey of the forces of nature, and his chances of remaining alive were minimal'. Later, and especially during the *early* industrial era, work was considered 'man's duty and lifted to the level of the most honoured human activity, until it became man's pride'. Then, in the late-industrial period, with the rise of the labour union and supporting national legislation, work became a right. Now, as Salvadori puts it, 'We are . . . witnessing the beginning of a situation in which work is no longer a right but a status symbol.'[3]

We have already reached the stage when the most highly skilled professionals work the longest hours and the least skilled labourers the shortest. If we should ever reach the stage when only 2 per cent (or 20 per cent, or even 50 per cent) of the employables can work, it will clearly be the men with the rarest skills who will hold jobs. The very fact of their being employed will confer high social status, reversing a long-standing rule of social ranking. What then is to become of the rest of us? In the early transition period, how will we deal with the sense of guilt that idleness will raise? The Calvinist ethic now assures us that idleness is the work of the devil and that work is virtuous. Under the initial impact of enforced unemployment, we shall have to create a new ethic to replace the mores that have so strongly dominated the Judeo-Christian world for so long.

And how will people spend their time? Some will find satisfying volunteer service roles in helping others. Some will find creative outlets in the arts, sports, and the more traditional leisure-time activities. But, in addition, *learning* may become the major non-paid occupation of large segments of the population. The signs are by now beginning to show in the expanding demand for adult educational programmes, the rapid growth of educational television, the sales boom in books and magazines, and the growing interest in music, theatre, and the traditional fine arts. A world that turns from making things to enjoying ideas may sound like a fantasy better suited to utopian or science-fiction literature than to responsible forecast. At this stage of things it is still too early to know how the librarians ought to classify it. It is as plausibly the one as the other.

It is equally plausible to expect a continuing rise in popular participation in politics and civic affairs. The long-term trend toward wider distribution of political power and active citizen involvement is being dramatically expressed today in the rebellions localized in the major cities of the world. The current search among the world's youth for meaningful forms of 'participant democracy' is being interpreted by some as a transitional crisis condition that will somehow eventually find a stable resolution. Others see it as a preliminary precursor of a continuing style of inter-generational confrontation. Again, either forecast is plausible.

In a world where machines will do more of our work and institutional change will be rapid, surely different forms of meaningful occupation must evolve. Already the concept of 'full employment' has been modified with the slow accretion of changing practices. Early retirement is displacing people from the labour force before their productive years have run out. Young people are entering the labour force at much later ages than their fathers, first devoting long periods to education. Their delayed entry is paid for in part by the scholarship systems. Britain already offers college grants to virtually everyone who can qualify for college. The United States may soon follow this example; even without universal grants, around 40 per cent of American youth receive some college training, and the proportion is rising rapidly. In California, it is now nearly 80 per cent. It is also true that the number of women in the labour force is also rising, particularly married women, more particularly well-educated married women whose children no longer require them at home. But that too may be in for a change as husbands' salaries rise sufficiently to provide satisfactory family incomes and as more women find productive voluntary outlets for their activities.

Few futurists doubt that family incomes will continue to rise far beyond the wage earners' present expectations:

Kahn and Wiener are using a middle-level projection of United States per capita income for the year 2000 of around $10,000, a trebling of the 1965 level of $3,500 in but 35 years. That is equivalent to a shift from around £1,400 to around £4,100 at current official exchange rates. With an annual average growth in Gross National Product (GNP) of 3 per cent in Britain, the 1966 per capita share of GNP would rise from about £590 to £1,400; at 4 per cent it would rise to over £2,000—well over trebled in 35 years. These are per capita estimates. Multiply them by a modest 4 members per family, and they suggest average family incomes in the year 2000 of the order of £16,000 in the United States and £5,600 in Britain at 3 per cent, and £8,120 at 4 per cent growth rates. Extend these forecasts an additional 20 years and the average family income levels jump to over £31,000 in the United States and between £10,500 and £15,500 in Britain—all expressed in constant purchasing power of money.

These are mean estimates and ignore the questions of income distribution. They are also unrefined forecasts, as any such long-range quantitative estimates inevitably must be. But they do suggest a new scale for our thinking. And they also suggest what happens when large numbers get compounded at even modest growth rates over a few decades.

These forecasts have been adjusted for population increase which is also subject to the effects of compound interest rates operating on large numbers. So to emphasize the point, it is necessary to consider what could happen to GNP itself over the next decades.

In 1966 Britain's GNP was around £32,500 million. At a 3 per cent growth rate that figure would more than double by the year 2000 to £84,400 million. At a 4 per cent growth rate it would nearly quadruple to £122,000 million. At a 5 per cent growth rate it would quintuple to £167,000 million. By present outlooks, a steady 5 per cent growth rate is unlikely, but an average rate somewhat between 3 per cent and 4 per cent is probably a reasonable expectation. For a rough and conservative guess, let us accept that the 1966 level of GNP—£32,500 million—will go to £100,000 million in the next 35 years; a modest trebling. Then consider the levels of public expenditure that will be possible, rather, that will be *necessary* to maintain economic stability. Consider how much can then be allocated to education, motorways, housing, national parks, health services, the British Museum, and so on.

These estimated figures indicate that we are on the verge of unprecedented wealth in the developed nations, a level of affluence that few of us can yet begin to imagine. When combined with the new wealth of knowledge that is forthcoming, this affluence is sure to generate new opportunities, new priorities, and new problems. We must all soon ask how we will be using this new-found wealth and, far more important, what that wealth will do to the highly developed nations where hundreds of thousands might still be poor, and to a world where thousands of millions of people in Asia, Africa, and Latin America will still be absolutely poor and relatively destitute.

Behind the GNP curve lies the recent explosion in the arts, the sciences, and the technologies. This is a world-wide phenomenon, even though it is still heavily localized in but a few nations. Because knowledge is peculiarly ignorant of national boundaries, the scientists, artists and technologists throughout the world have come to share a common body of information, theory and method. They share a

33

consensus on values and on the epistemological bases for valuation. In effect they share a common culture.

Unlike the commodities of other enterprises, knowledge has the peculiar properties of drawing upon infinite resources, of being infinitely expandable, and being enriched by consumption. Given the incentives of impelling intellectual pursuits, and barring political or celestial catastrophe, we can expect that the current knowledge explosion will continue. More, we can be confident that it will continue to expand at exponential rates. As more and more people tune into the knowledge channels—whether as students in organized schools, as workers in the knowledge industries, or as persons seeking an avocational substitute for paid work—we can also expect that rising proportions of the populations will share the non-national culture of the present intellectual elites.

The internationalizing effect of science is being abetted by the parallel internationalizing effect of the communications systems that science and technology have spawned. Men who follow the intellectual pursuits are now able to maintain virtually instantaneous contact with each other. As the speed of communication and transportation rise and as the costs fall, the links that unite them are being further strengthened. These links are not new ones, of course. For several hundred years men have been able to stay in touch with each other around the globe. What *is* new is the speed of communication that is now commonplace, the intimacy that high accessibility provokes, and the extension of these communication lines to nearly the whole of the Western world's population.

Although it has been commonplace to note that radio, television and jet airplanes have shrunk the world to a small fraction of its nineteenth century size, the scale is still so new that the consequences to society of that contraction are nonetheless still obscure. For example, student revolts around the world certainly cannot be attributed simply to the communications channels that have united the students into a common movement of protest, but those channels were nonetheless a necessary condition to the scenario that has evolved.

Throughout, there can be little doubt about the influence that radio, telephone and particularly television has had upon similar movements of social protest. Television has the powerful capacity for turning distant events into local ones, for breaking through language barriers, and for communicating meaning as well as information. As its coverage extends to larger spectra of events and to larger numbers of people, it cannot fail to introduce an international unifying force with qualities never available in the world before. Real-time and realistic communication among such diverse places as Morningside Heights, Boulevard St Michel, and the suburbs of Saigon has a way of turning these places into neighbourhoods within the same city.

Another effect of shrinking space and time has been the recent rise of the international business firm that makes the services of its head-quarters' technical staff promptly available to all its branches, wherever they may be. Those global corporate networks are rapidly being bound together by data-transmission lines feeding into head-quarters' computers that will further erode regional differences in products and practices. In turn corporate mergers are creating smaller numbers of giants that span nations, further integrating the world-wide economy and speeding up the processes of modernization.

The international revolution of rising expectations, the inter-national student movement, and the international business firms are but the more visible signs of the spatially extensive communities that span nations. They are being paralleled by growing networks of informal organizations that join individuals and groups who share interests. These are perhaps best typified by the contemporary in-visible colleges—those loose collections of colleagues which become visible whenever and wherever their members happen to gather, but whose real locations are inside the communication channels their members inhabit. They are typified, too, in the societies of hippies, musicians and diplomats who similarly share cultures with others who are spatially dispersed. The spatial extent of these culturally defined communities is spreading rapidly, as the pace of cultural diffusion rises: witness the speed with which fashions in clothes, politics, and architecture get transplanted from one corner of the world to others.

But the internationalizing trends do not necessarily mean that the world is becoming homogenized: just the opposite is happening. There can be no doubt that nationalism is on the rise at the same time that the cultural and economic boundaries of nations are becoming more permeable. So, too, is regionalism, at the same time that national governments and national pride are becoming stronger. Indeed, so too is localism, as the current community-organization drives in both the American suburbs and central city ghettos suggest.

It looks as though we are evolving a very ambiguous and complex sort of place-related social organization, in which groups joined by common interests are finding coherence against a wide range of spatial scales. Similarly, we are evolving a very complex network of interest bonds that are defining voluntary communities of ever more diverse sorts. Put another way, the rising scale of the society, the increased ease of communication, and hence the emergence of a world society is making for a range of cultural diversity that has never been possible before.

It was pre-industrial society that was homogeneous. Members of village communities followed similar life styles, shared common beliefs, and conformed to traditional behavioural norms. Members of the new high-scale world society have the opportunity to choose among a multiplicity of options. They can selectively join any of thousands of sub-groups, each with its own styles and value systems. They can selectively read in an ever-expanding literature, follow any of a growing number of religions and, for the near-future at least, choose careers from among a widening range of possibilities. The numbers of such options have been expanding during the industrial era. Nothing appears to suggest that this long-term trend will be diverted. Increasing affluence, higher levels of education, and rapid social change are all likely to accelerate the trend to diversity— despite the shrinkage of the globe. I am suggesting that the forecasts of a mass-society are likely to prove wrong. Growing diversity in a growing society will have the inevitable effect of turning what would otherwise be small minorities into large and potentially powerful ones. Post-industrial society is likely to comprise a pluralism of competing minorities, with far less conformity than any in the history of the planet.

The shape of the world-population growth curve over the millennia is well known, as are the frightening extrapolations into the future. There were about one-quarter billion people in the world at the time of Christ, one-half billion at the time the American colonies were being established, one billion in 1850, two billion in 1925, and there will be around four billion in the mid-1970s. The consensus forecast has been putting it at around six billion in the year 2000. But it may then stabilize there. Donald Bogue reports that the impact of contraception during the past few years has already reversed the long-term trend, and that the rate of population growth has been slackening since 1965. He is predicting that 'from 1965 onward . . . the rate of world population growth may be expected to decline with each passing year. The rate of growth will slacken at such a pace that it will be zero or near zero at about the year 2000, so that population growth will not be regarded as a major social problem except in isolated and small "retarded" areas.'[4]

If his projection is nearer right than the straight extrapolative ones, and it seems that it is, then one of the two major doomsday threats will be eroded away. But the problems that accompany population growth will not disappear.

The poor and populous nations of the world have been losing

ground steadily, relative to the levels of living that are emerging in the highly developed nations. Because population growth rates in the African, Asian, and Latin American nations are likely to respond more slowly to the contraceptive revolution, their status will be relatively worse in the future than now, despite even acceleration in rates of economic development there. At the same time, levels of literacy, aspiration, and international political influence are likely to continue to rise, providing the makings for a new scale of international conflict among the have and have-not nations on an unprecedented scale. Needless to say, those latent conflicts will be exacerbated by the visible contrasts that television and air travel will expose.

Richard Meier has recently been projecting the future patterns of city growth in Asia and finds no way of avoiding forecasts of city sizes up to 40 million.[5] A few years ago Kingsley Davis prepared a forecast for Calcutta and concluded that the metropolitan area may have 36 to 66 million by the year 2000.[6] In contrast, nineteenth century Manchester might have been a very amiable environment, and twenty-first century Manchester may strike many as a very attractive alternative. It is likely that the city expansion processes in the less developed nations are going to push immigration policy up to the top of the policy agenda in the more developed ones.

Similarly, the disparities in stages of development within the developed nations are likely to generate the major domestic policy problems there. As measured against any absolute index of quality, life in the contemporary city is far more comfortable and far less riven by hardship than at any time in the past. Even at its worst, housing is cleaner, safer, and more sanitary than it was, say, at the start of this century. Hours of work have been cut dramatically. Disease rates have been drastically reduced; for some dread diseases they have been reduced to zero. Education levels have been raised for virtually all segments of the population. Incomes are up to levels that permit a quality of nutrition never before achieved by national populations at large. On all these indices, the future promises even more dramatic improvements.

And yet we are approaching the end of the century with large proportions of Western populations living in poverty—poverty relative to current national norms and to current national capabilities. If poverty is defined as family incomes below half the national median, then the poor comprise twenty per cent of the United States population today and about 16–17 per cent in Britain. The combined effects of the various changes mentioned above do not necessarily mean that their relative status will improve during the next decades.

In the absence of concerted efforts to counteract these effects, it is likely that those who are now poor will be relatively worse off than they are now, mirroring the growing relative deprivation of those in the less developed nations.

Those who have the social and cognitive skills that will permit entry into the affluent sectors of post-industrial society are likely to fare very well indeed during the next generations. Those who lack these skills may find the entry points are closed. In the short run, employers can be expected to demand higher and higher levels of education and training. In the United States even clerks are now being required to have twelve years of schooling, and to present themselves in middle-class modes of dress, behaviour, and speech. A growing proportion of occupations requires college-level preparation. Admission into the modern credential-society is becoming increasingly difficult. It is more difficult, in turn, to find positive roles that also confer a sense of personal dignity.

Many in America who still live in pre-industrial status and who have so far been excluded from industrial society have recently been indignantly demanding that they too have access to the modern world. The recent wave of riots is the most outspoken statement of their dilemma. The American experience has not yet been repeated in the other developed nations, where poverty also persists, but where working-class status carries dignity and stability. One wonders, however, whether the present American experience may be an early-warning of future European experience. At this moment in history, America is closest to the post-industrial stage of development. When the European nations and Japan reach that stage in the 1970s and 1980s, can we expect that working-class groups will maintain their present stability? From this perspective it looks as if this is the critical question for urban planners. Today, America's central urban policy issue is posed by the dilemma of a large pre-industrial, city-based population in a society about to leave the industrial age. It could soon happen here in Britain as well.

SOME IMPLICATIONS FOR CITY PLANNING

There are a great many other portents of the future that we might have recorded here: the revolution under way in biology and the new possibilities for extending life spans and for genetic engineering, communication prospects that lasers are promising, possibilities for new kinds of air-supported and electrically propelled vehicles, new prospects for weather control, and so on. I have mentioned just a few of the prospects not with the intent of portraying what the future may be like, but rather as a way of suggesting that the social, political and economic environments for urban life may be in for some quantum changes. If they are, then our concept of future time will also have to change, and with it, our perceptions of our professional roles.

The conception of the future that has been guiding the city planning movement in the past is different from the one emerging in the new explorations. City planning has never really been orientated to future change. Despite the long horizons and the utopian traditions that have marked this field throughout its history, it has been guided by a future-directed ideology that has looked backwards; our binoculars have had an extra set of prisms built-in, so that, when we have aimed them at the future, they have reversed the field of vision.

I find it a sobering reminder, for example, that virtually not one of us foresaw the current affluence. No one foresaw the effects of widespread automobile ownership—whether on suburbanization, on the changing functions of the central business districts, or on the ways in which people would use their leisure time.

This is understandable for, instead of systematic forecasts of social change, we have prepared portraits of desired long-range futures for the physical-spatial city, because those portraits were for cities that would be built in the image of the long-range past. With genuinely bold and daring leadership, typically with selfless devotion to the public welfare, we have been proposing designs for future cities that were frequently idealized reconstructions of pre-industrial towns that served pre-industrial societies. I am reminded of the numerous attempts to build locally scaled social neighbourhoods in contemporary American cities; the post-war 'self-contained' new towns in Britain; the anti-auto ideology, and the persisting efforts to reconstruct in industrial democratic societies the kinds of large-scale urban designs that characterized the monarchies of pre-industrial times.

None of us has yet thought through the coming effects on cities and urban societies that now lie implicit in new electronic-communication systems, computers, rising per capita wealth, place-free and low-cost nuclear energy, new air-borne transport systems, new modes of retail distribution, new public-private non-profit corporations, the new movements for participatory democracy, and so on. Nor have we felt the need to, for we have been conducting our affairs against a concept of the future and against a set of substantive models that have not called for these sorts of *qualitative* conjectures.

City planners early adopted the thoughtways and the analytical methods that engineers devised for the design of public works, and they then applied them to the design of cities. In that context, and in the sense that city plans take a long time to accomplish, our work has indeed been future-orientated.

Seeking a scale on future 'requirements', in the engineering model, we have always attempted to make good long-range quantitative forecasts of the population sizes that the cities must accommodate. Recently we have acquired some considerable skill in forecasting future travel volumes, as a way of scaling future demand for highways. In this sense, too, our work has been future-orientated.

But our plans and scalar forecasts have typically been made against a series of assumptions and on modes of prediction that the new futurists are beginning to challenge. These assumptions include at least the following:

1. That social organization and social objectives will remain stable during the time-period under review.
2. That there is a society-wide consensus on city-development goals.
3. Because these goals are stable, future goals will be like present goals, and that they are knowable by professionals.

The recent projective studies have made the first two of these assumptions highly questionable. If history is indeed at a turning point without prior precedent, and if cultural diversity is really on the rise, present patterns may not guide us well. These studies suggest that projections of qualitative change must precede quantitative forecasts. They suggest that extrapolations of past trends are no longer reasonable, if only because extrapolation implies that past determinants of trend lines will persist into the future. Similarly they point to some built-in deficiencies of our present quantitative methods. The traditional scientific canons cannot be formally applied to phenomena that cannot yet be either observed or measured; and that plays havoc with empirically derived parameters. Qualitative projection requires reasoned judgment—built upon rigorous theory when it exists, but openly speculative and conjectural when it does not.

The third assumption—that professionals can make decent judgments on future societal *objectives* by observing present ones—a central issue in all planning fields, is even more dubious. First, because so much of the future is unpredictable; second, because professionals are inherently plagued by so many biases that inhibit their comprehension of the wants of increasingly diverse minorities. I shall argue in Part II of this article that a great many decisions that professionals are accustomed to take are best left to the public itself.

I shall also contend that we have frequently asked the wrong questions and sought to control the wrong variables. In the city planning field, for example, we have been asking questions about optimum city size and about optimum city form. Yet, the shifts in recent and future interaction patterns suggest that settlement size is no longer a critical question. For increasing segments of the high-scale societies, it is no longer meaningful. Similarly, questions about over-all metropolitan spatial arrangements are giving way to the more intricate ones concerned with inter-establishment linkages and the ranges of locational opportunity open to types of families and firms. Rather than the design of physical lay-outs of cities, the city planning task is turning to the design of the fiscal and institutional arrangements that might then control the city-building process and to the designs for social services. The detailed decisions can be left to the consumer.

And then the prime questions that will be raised by the move into post-industrialism are: who is to pay? who is to profit? and who is to decide? The fruits of the coming affluence will inevitably be unequally distributed, and that is likely to become the dominant political fact of the time. It could well be that the distributional questions will also be the dominant ones for city planning.

It could also be that the political urgency of these questions will force an expansion of city planning's traditional preoccupation with the quality of the city to encompass the larger range of concerns with the quality of urban life. Even with a rising flow of wealth through both public and private channels, we shall still have deliberately to plan for the expansion of opportunity and personal freedom. The future is no more likely to be beneficent than perverse and tyrannical. Futurists have written both sorts of scenarios, and they are equally plausible.

In our traditional lines of work, we shall soon have to confront the dilemma posed by the huge sunk investment in the nineteenth and twentieth century cities. The physical plant that future generations will inherit is not likely to match their standards of acceptable quality or their capacities to buy better cities. Buildings and roads have too long a life-span to suit the pace of historical change. The Americans dealt with that fact by simply leaving the old cities behind, and moving out to new settlements in the suburbs. That solved the individuals' problems, but left a social residue unresolved. How will the great cities of Europe deal with old plants that were built in the industrial age?

On the other side of that coin we shall have to confront the dilemma posed, on the one hand, by our fiscal capacities for building an amiable and beautiful environment and the public pressures to build quickly and, on the other, by the paucity of ideas with which to

41

meet that challenge. The fitting criteria of aesthetic quality are not likely to be those that have guided urban designers in the past. Those persons who will be able to afford spaciousness and high geographic mobility will also be able to claim both, and these cannot be simultaneously supplied in the mediaeval, or nineteenth century, or even the twentieth century packages we have been offering. Multi-house and multi-car families will use far more space than we are accustomed to provide; and those demands will be met, whether we co-operate or not. At the same time, and integral with the city designs, they will be demanding opportunities for exciting educational activities, for productive social roles, and for an information-rich life. These opportunities, too, must also be created as necessities—at least as imperative as sewers and streets.

These will be calling for a speculative and inventive capacity that has been rare in our field. If Professor Brzezinski and the others are right about the degree of qualitative change that is before us, we shall find few guides by looking to the cities of the past. As Britton Harris has been contending, we shall have to invent the future city and the opportunities for a rich urban life, because the models have not yet emerged in the course of past history.[7]

There is likely to be a happy congruence between the expanding knowledge of human and social systems, and our capacity to plan for this congruence. Planning has until recently been only an idea. With improving theory and improving computational capability, planning is only now becoming an operational method for defining goals, reaching decisions, and taking actions. In the post-industrial era it is likely to become the normal mode of decision and action—in a wide array of human activities. We are now learning how to apply the idea of planning to the city. And when we do, it may well be that our most troubling questions will surround the issues of equity. The industrial age was dominated by the idea of efficiency. The post-industrial age is likely to be dominated by conflicts over equity. The over-riding question for planners will be 'how shall the social product of an increasingly affluent and increasingly capable society be distributed?' Or, as I put it above: 'Who shall pay?, who shall profit?, and who shall decide?'

Part II: Permissive Planning

In Part I of this paper it was suggested that the rapid onset of the post-industrial stage of development is likely to force two major changes in urban planning. One anticipated change is substantive:

42

the increasing pace of history is revealing a new set of problems, different in kind from those that have been occupying city planners. During the industrial age, the profession's work was aimed at improving the cities' efficiency. In the imminent post-industrial age, unprecedented wealth will turn the equity issues into imperatives. Growing disparities in levels of wealth and welfare among increasingly diverse publics are likely to engender severe conflicts both within the highly developed nations and between the wealthy and the poor nations.

The other major change is largely procedural. New developments in the social and behavioural sciences are increasing our understanding of societal systems—of their component economies, polities, communities, families and geographies. A consequence of the new theory is a growing capacity to predict future changes in these systems. We are now quickly accumulating the skills for *planning* and then for *engineering* social change.

This could be a highly felicitous development. But it could also be the basis for a new tyranny of technocrats. Already the specialists operating the simulation systems are finding it difficult, sometimes impossible, even to talk to politicians. The concepts they work with are unfamiliar, and the techniques they use seem mysterious. Decision-makers are increasingly forced to accept the conclusions of technical specialists, thus putting the specialists in the role of governors. As the planning technologies grow more complex and as the distribution of information and analytical skills shifts from politicians to technicians, there is likely also to be a redistribution of political power. It now looks as though the post-industrial period will be marked by a new style of government. Dominated by the idea and methods of planning, the coming decades will bring new possibilities for creative confrontation with the future.

This part of the paper focuses upon some questions surrounding the relations between technics and politics as they might affect city planning. As before, my observations and comments are limited to the American scene. What happens there has implications for what happens elsewhere, but these interpretations I must leave to the reader. With that disclaimer, let me simply state my thesis with the aim of making it explicit ahead of time.

City planning has not yet adopted either the planning idea or the planning method. It has instead internalized the concepts and methods of design from civil engineering and architecture. In the post-industrial period, when planning will be the characteristic mode of deciding and acting, city planning is likely to adopt a rationalistic posture with respect to valuation and to future change, displacing its traditional ideological posture. It will thus increase its power, including the power to help some groups and to hurt others. If city planning also carries over some of its traditional roles and self-images, the exercise of its new-found power will unwittingly hurt just those groups that are least able to help themselves. To counter that implicit danger, we shall need built-in procedures for *valuating* the wants of increasingly diverse publics and for *evaluating* the planned actions to test whether these actually do serve the valued ends.

THE IDEA OF PLANNING

I shall be using the term 'planning' to refer to a special way of deciding and acting. The minimum necessary conditions of the planning method are these:

1. The explication of goals, objectives and targets for each sub-system under consideration including, in the public sphere, each of the publics that will be touched by the planned actions.
2. The continuous forecasting of both qualitative and quantative changes that lie outside the planners' control.
3. The continuous forecasting of likely chains of consequences, within and especially among subsystems, resulting from each set of alternatively hypothesized planned actions.
4. The appraisal of investment costs and welfare pay-offs attached to each alternatively projected history. If a reasonable fit is found between an hypothesized course of action and the value sets, a time-sequenced action strategy is synthesized, comprising shorter-run action tactics, each with its timed targets. Each shorter-run tactic is carefully appraised for its likely net return, and is then expressed in the language of fiscal budgets.
5. The continuous monitoring of the systems being planned. A constant flow of information on actual outcomes is fed back into the planning system to signal forecasting errors and to actuate corrective steps. In addition, early warning of imminent danger or opportunity can alert deciders and, most important, the effectiveness of goal-directed actions can be empirically evaluated for each subsystem and each public.

The distinguishing marks of the planning approach to decision and action are, then, its explicit goals basis, its evaluation of alternative futures and alternative future courses of action, and its reliance upon feedback of outcomes and pay-offs. Planning is *inherently* oriented to outputs, such as public services and facilities,

44

as *investments* which have ascertainable pay-offs to client publics, As such, planning is essentially an *economizing* approach to the future, constantly appraising trade-offs among alternative investment strategies in search of the desired welfare returns.

This is certainly a highly idealized conception of a planning process. As an ideal, it is unattainable. But it is an ideal worth pursuing, for we profit as we approach it. At the present stage in its history, city planning has made but small headway toward this ideal.

Two Competing Traditions

Two sources have stimulated the city planning movement and have shaped its development. The one, an offspring of the German Rationalization and the scientific management movements, cast city planning in the role of the city engineer who sought to improve efficiency in the city's physical plant. The other, an offspring of the earlier social reform movements, cast it in the role of the social reformer who sought to improve the lot of people living in the cities. The parent of both sources was, of course, the industrial revolution that emptied the farms, crowded the cities, and generated a new society plagued by the problems of adapting to rapid change. Both sources have exerted continuing, albeit competing, influence during this century, but the engineering approach has been dominant.

With the rise of the factory system, populations became concentrated in the cities that housed the new industries; the cities themselves, however, grew in pre-industrial patterns. City engineering and city planning developed as attempts to exploit available city-building technologies and, later, to invent new ones. As a result men soon learned how to dispose of wastes, to supply sanitary water, to build intra-city transportation systems, to provide schools and hospitals, and even to build tolerable housing of some quality for everyone.

These were no modest successes. We have only to look to the Calcuttas of the contemporary world to appreciate how far we have come. Despite the many inadequacies of present-day Western cities, we must surely agree that their record is impressive. To be sure, we have yet to solve air-, water-, and noise-pollution problems; housing quality does not begin to match our technological capabilities; and no city has yet disposed of traffic congestion. But the early objectives have been won. Epidemics of the dread diseases are gone. Obnoxious spill-overs from factories to adjacent houses have been largely eliminated. Producers are accessible to their suppliers and customers, and retail outlets are accessible to residents. The majority of the cities' residents *can* live with a sense of decency and some even with

45

dignity. Our cities *do* work. If we knew how to measure their overall efficiency, they would probably score pretty high.

Much of that success reflects the comparative simplicity of the problems inherent in the early industrial city. The early city planners could properly consider that solutions to problems stood in direct, one-to-one relation to demonstrated causes—typhoid to a water-carried salmonella, traffic breakdowns to unpaved muddy streets, rodent infestations to accumulated garbage, and so on. The science of the time supplied the explanations that, in turn, led to direct technical solutions. So long as there was consensus on objectives, there was little doubt about the actions to be taken.

The critical step in that process is the epistemological one—the concept that cause and effect are directly related—such that causes of problems can be identified and that correct and direct solutions can be found. This was a reasonable presumption for the kinds of problems being treated in those early days. Because the systems being dealt with could be conceived as being effectively independent, unilateral intervention was initially sufficient. Recourse to the planning method was, therefore, unnecessary.

Later, when the massive problems had been alleviated, when the cities' structures had grown more complex, when ever more refined solutions were sought, and when demands for amenities replaced the easier demands for removal of obstacles—it was then recognized that the workings of the city's physical parts really did affect each other. Engineers and planners began to design sets of systems, searching for overall city plans that would simultaneously attack a number of problems. The step was an important one, for it laid the foundations of the systems-analysis and systems-design efforts that permit positive invention of desired future states while also alleviating undesired present conditions.

Taming of the massive problems came just when incomes were rising rapidly and when cultural urbanization was making for cultural diversity among the cities' residents. Those who wanted and could afford better environmental qualities were able to lay claim to them. The overall city plans reflected this growing search for amenity.

At this juncture the technical problem-solving concepts of the engineer merged with the aspiration-raising efforts of the social reformer. It may have been at this juncture also that city planning split off from city engineering, for the engineers typically remained subsystem specialists while the city planners sought to become system-wide generalists. However wide the split, though, the thought-ways of the engineer continued to dominate the work of the system-wide planners. Although city planning has by now developed a professional subculture and although its practitioners profess social purposes far beyond the resolution of current and discrete problems, the city planning movement, I believe, has never outgrown its intellectual origins in city engineering and architecture. The original premises underpinning civic-works design became overlaid with a social ideology that introduced different purposes, but the premises remained in an epistemological eclecticism that continues to mark the trade today. Engineering contributed an operational style and social ideology contributed the purposive rationale for applying that style as a substitute for market processes. But still the idea of planning never got built into the profession's work.

Social Ideology's Influence on Early City Planning

The ideology arose in response to the horrid living conditions and physical squalor of the early industrial city, but it was more than a reflection of moral indignation. Aimed at effecting fundamental social change, it was a positive credo that was inextricably caught up in the main current of American thought and thus shared in a complex network of beliefs. Despite the danger of over-simplification, we can identify a few of the major precepts that have been shaping the city planning movement.[8]

1. The city was thought to be unnatural and inherently unhealthy and immoral. In order to counteract its intrinsically evil character, it had to be remoulded to resemble the country town that had preceded it.
2. Especially in America, where immigrants from other parts of the world were considered 'strange' and were seen as a threat to the social order, an effort had to be made to acculturate them. At this time, when the idea of physical environmental determinism was at its peak, the central strategy for turning immigrants into middle-class, stable citizens was to provide them with a middle-class physical environment.
3. In parallel, the middle- and upper-class supporters and leaders of the movement were confident that they knew what was best, both for the migrants to the city and for society at large. They therefore selflessly inaugurated a variety of governmental and philanthropic enterprises, designed to improve the conditions of city life. Anticipating similar contemporary efforts by many decades, they substituted a collective rationality for traditional individual rationality, placing decision-making in the hands of those elite groups who were both informed and oriented to the public interest.

47

4. At the time these efforts were being made, many city governments in America were controlled by political machines, and
   they had indeed become corrupt. The reformers were, therefore,
   determined to keep their programmes out of politics. Their
   tactic was at first also to keep them out of government. But
   that soon became unnecessary, for it was found that technical
   professionalism in government was a more effective way of
   keeping politics out of government.
5. In the spirit of successful captains of industry, the programmes
   for betterment were launched with the bold optimism that
   wilful action could control future outcomes: the city, like the
   factory, could be designed to accord with deliberate purpose.
   It was at this point that the teleologic and utopian outlook was
   implanted within city planning, nearly a century ahead of the
   the recent futurists and planners.

In brief, then, we can typify the early ideology of the American
city planning movement as anti-city, elitist, apolitical, rationalistic,
sometimes technocratic, but always oriented to an image of the
larger public welfare. As direct descendants of the Enlightenment
the early city planners were out to perfect history.

Surely these were responses to the failure of market processes that
controlled construction and use of buildings and space. The general
reaction of urban social reformers was to bring the markets to
account.

Two major strategies were pursued. The first was to replace
market processes by administered governmental programmes. The
second was to constrain market behaviour in an effort to prevent
the more outrageous outcomes, by setting limits on the builders and
landowners who were profiteering from the city-building bonanza,
typically at the expense of the poor. The tactic applied to both strategies was essentially the same. It was, as already noted, to substitute
for individual rationality the collective rationality of public-spirited
and knowledgeable professionals working inside city government.

These efforts to regulate market processes were in part impelled
by an ideological opposition to markets and, in some sectors of the
movement, by a distrust of private businessmen. At the time the
movement was being organized, though, I suspect it was largely
motivated by a recognition that the market was failing to perform as
classical economics had promised it would. Pursuing the belief that
governments could simply force greedy businessmen to act in the
public interest, social reformers adopted the tactics of regulation and
direct public enterprise.

Rationales for Governmental Intervention

The early planners' actions were taken intuitively and without the theoretic supports their successors can draw upon. By now a considerable body of theory has been accumulated in welfare economics and elsewhere that supplies partial credence to the earlier strategies, while simultaneously raising some doubts. We can here simply catalogue several classes of conditions that have been identified as warrants for governmental intervention; later we can examine their relevance to city planning activities.

It is now understood that, in their very nature, markets are incapable of dealing with certain kinds of economic transactions:

First, they are incapable of supplying those goods and services for which it is either impossible or too difficult for a private seller to charge a price and for which he cannot exclude non-paying customers. These, the so-called 'pure public-goods', have the peculiarities that (a) if they are supplied to one, they are thereby supplied to all, and (b) it costs no more to supply an additional person. Since it is costless to serve more customers, social product would be reduced by constraining consumption, and governments have thus been wont to offer these goods and services. The classic example is the lighthouse, but there are a great many more—radio broadcasting, mosquito elimination, streets and highways, and national defence are also pure public goods. If governments or philanthropists did not supply them, they would probably not be supplied at all.

A *second* class of public goods is also impossible to price properly in the market because the consumer does not receive *all* the benefits that arise from his having consumed it. 'External' (social) benefits are realized by others who do not themselves use the service, so the seller cannot charge the buyer at a price that reflects the total social value received. For example, a person treated for a communicable disease gets relief, but others in the neighbourhood also benefit by having their risks reduced. It would be virtually impossible for the physician to collect from the neighbours, and so public-health departments have typically had to take over the function, charging the whole neighbourhood through taxes.[9]

A *third* situation, involving rather the opposite sort of transaction, has been a major cause of governmental regulation in the urban field. These are dealings that result in negative external effects, that is, social costs, such that neighbours have to bear the costs of someone else's valued activity. For example, a factory dumps waste into a river that a town downstream uses for municipal purposes. The town must now treat its water supply, but there is no market mechanism by which it can charge the factory for the purification costs. If the factory is to be made to pay those bills, or, alternatively, if it is to be prevented from generating the social costs, the terms must be set outside the market system. Again, government is the only effective agency for dealing with the situation.

Fourth, governments are encouraged to enter business directly when wanted goods are not forthcoming from private enterprise. Some lines of business are just not feasible in the private sector, either because the scale of investment required exceeds available private funding or because the risks involved are too great to entice private capital. Launching vehicles for communications satellites certainly illustrate the first, and probably the second as well. Governments can afford to undertake large and risky investments that private corporations cannot. Modern governments in the Western world do not go bankrupt—they only change management.

A *fifth* rationale for public intervention into markets involves the condition, increasingly common in highly integrated societies, in which all persons may profit more if *each* agrees to yield certain of his rights. In this situation a government agency serving as referee facilitates the exchange of information so that all concerned can avoid the hazards attendant upon mutual ignorance of plans. The willingness of the banking community to accept the edicts issued by the central banks is one clear instance; the traffic signal is another; urban renewal programmes are notable ones. Governmental economic stabilization programmes are by far the most dramatic and successful ones. (These are all in the nature of non-zero-sum games in which the the total winnings are greater if free market play is constrained.)

A *sixth* situation, closely related, is the circumstance in which private investors acting in accordance with their own relatively short-run calculus of profitability would deprive the public of certain long-run benefits. If, for example, the public values the *future* benefits of a forest more highly than the timber industry (technically, the public applies a lower future-discounting rate), it has the choice of buying the forest and preserving it as a park. Again, when governments' time-horizons have been longer and their discount rates lower than private owners', they have sometimes simply passed laws prohibiting owners from using their resources freely.

Seventh, governmental powers are commonly invoked to prohibit individuals from behaving in self-destructive ways when government judges it can command better information about what is harmful to individuals than can the individuals themselves. Thus, thalidomide and other drugs have been banned. Drawing on the same rationale, government has justified less clear-cut prohibitions, making the use of marijuana a criminal offence and imposing censorship on films and books. (In the United States many local governments go much further, having thick statute books aimed at protecting people from their own immorality and from their inherited propensities to sin.)

The *eighth* case is the obverse of the seventh. Governmental regulations are designed to force or encourage individuals to engage in *healthful* behaviour. Children must attend school for a mandatory number of years; in communities which have fluoridated water supplies, all residents must partake of this benefit (unless, of course, they purchase bottled water). Almost all government programmes aimed at positive self-improvement are permissive and encouraging, however, rather than mandatory. The parks, recreation, theatre, and arts programmes are notable examples.

Ninth, government has sometimes required individuals either to refrain from self-injurious, or to engage in healthful, behaviour because the *short-run* general public welfare would thereby be improved. This rationale, resembling both the second (the social-benefit case) and the sixth (long-range public benefit), is currently popular in city-planning circles. It is exemplified by architectural control—the imposition of aesthetic standards on new buildings, with the aim of improving the city's visual qualities. The increased costs are borne solely by the builders; external benefits (social benefits) are received by the passing publics at no cost.

These nine circumstances suggest that there are indeed conditions in which markets cannot work at all, others in which the social product is increased if government engages in certain enterprises, and still others where regulatory procedures might assure higher returns to all individual consumers. We could catalogue a longer list, of course, but this inventory will serve our present purposes. I shall later want to mention circumstances in which market-type systems attached to governmental enterprises might better regulate the production and distribution of community services.

The Civil Engineering Style

In seeking to confront market insufficiencies, city planners early adopted the techniques of civil engineers rather than those of economists. In so doing, they were remarkably inventive. Their major social inventions were the *technical standard*, which set minimum permissible levels of quality; the *master plan*, which set forth overall system design; and the *land-use regulation*, which constrained the locational decisions of individual establishments. These techniques were derived directly from civil engineering; the innovation lay in translating the language of engineering manuals and contracts-and-specifications into governmental laws and regulations. The aim was basically to accomplish in the market place the sorts of deliberate outcomes that are readily accomplished in the centralized decision-setting of an engineer-client relationship or a centrally controlled government enterprise.

This was a quixotic aim, for the city planners paid scant attention to the realities of three major differences between a public market place and a centralized-decision milieu. First, market outcomes are shaped by the actions of thousands of decision-makers, whereas individual buildings are typically designed by only a few. Secondly, market outcomes represent the vector of innumerable valuations by individuals, each behaving in accordance with his own peculiar value bases, in contrast to the usual consensus that marks an engineering work. And thirdly, the cumulated actions of many deciders work *non*-teleologically, shaping the development patterns of a multiplicity of subsystems, often in subtle and imperfectly understood ways. In contrast, decisions on specific civil projects are typically rationalistic, aimed at accomplishing limited ends for single subsystems.

Three concepts underlying the standards-regulations approach thus need to be re-examined: (1) that there is a meaningful community comprising all residents of a city or conurbation, who hold to and are bound together by a coherent value system; (2) that technical requirements and standards can be discovered that conform to and further those value systems; and (3) that we can conceive a system-wide, city-development policy that is technically valid and that will promote the overall community's interest.

I suggest that the first two are untenable and that the third is unattainable. But the third can stand as an ideal objective, worth pursuing if, but only if, the first two propositions are rejected. However, to reject the current conceptions of community and of standards is also to reject the foundations of the present operational style in city planning, and that will call for a reconstruction of the field.

Community Values

Insofar as there is a city-wide community—that is, a community of persons who share common interests about the city system—it

52

occupies at most but a small part of their attention. It is true enough that everyone living within a single watershed, for example, shares an interest in water supply and flood hazards. But, except during crises, such shared interests are relegated to the far corners of one's concerns, partly because we learned long ago to manage most of those systems.

Most of the place-defined communities to which people belong are small, typically comprising residents living within a few blocks. We have recently been learning something about these local, place-defined communities, and we are beginning to understand how elastic they are, how dramatically their size varies with social class, and how relatively unimportant they are among the many communities to which people belong. As suggested in Part I, the communities most valued by city residents are the thousands of different social groups that are bound together by voluntary association based on common interests attached to occupation, family, religion, hobby, or shared belief. These social communities are non-territorial in character, bringing people together from various localities.

Each social community is held together by a body of values peculiar to itself, and its value-set may put it in direct competition with other communities. Those persons who value open park-space, wherever it or they may be located, are ready to unite in defence of parks at the first sign of a highway-alignment plan; the social communities of people who like redwood trees are the nemesis of the highway engineer and housebuilder. The organized and informal communities of motorists are partial to highways, almost irrespective of alignment; a proposed route would pit them against the park-loving community. And so on. There has been so much written about the so-called 'metropolitan problem' and the 'metropolitan community' in America that we have accepted these catchphrases as though they referred to something real. The location-defined community, I suggest, claims at most but a small segment of the loyalties, interests, and concerns of city dwellers. If true, then the second concept—that technical standards conforming to community-wide goals can be found—is also doubtful.

Efficiency Versus Distribution

Every public action generates both efficiency effects and redistribution effects. Engineers have traditionally been alert to the former—the influence of highway alignment on travel costs, the effect of building materials on construction costs, the effects of separating sanitary from storm sewers on the costs of operating a sewage treatment plant. These efficiency effects are internal to the functioning of the subsystems being designed.

There are also *external* efficiency effects, such as the consequences of a flood-control project or a highway project on subsequent settlement patterns. Modern planning technologies are now making it possible to use such public works' subsystems deliberately in shaping land-development subsystems within the larger, city-wide system. If we could determine what arrangement of transportation facilities would fit well with what spatial arrangement of economic activities and residence-based activities, we could then test alternative transportation plans for their internal and external efficiencies. This important task is now occupying transportation planners, land planners, education planners, and economic planners; all are seeking to improve investment efficiencies in their respective fields by tracing the external effects on the economic development of nations. Although we can be optimistic about our growing capabilities thus to improve both internal and external efficiencies of the systems we operate upon, it will not be enough.

In addition to improving the workability of the city's components, every public action also shifts the distribution of benefits and costs among the various segments of the population. These redistributive consequences, commonly external to the subsystem being planned, affect various non-client groups, each in different ways and to different degrees.

The current attention to 'community values' in the Western world is being largely generated by the external distributional effects. It is not a debate over whether a new motorway box or a new airport conflicts with some holistic objective of the 'metropolitan community'. That community is largely mythical. Rather, it is a debate over which publics are to pay and which are to profit from the government's action.

It is fruitless—and certainly misleading—to compute overall community values. In a complex urban society there is no viable single community. And, because each of a multiplicity of competing communities values things against different value scales, there can be no set of generalized values or criteria against which to appraise a project. There can be only a plurality of competing values held by a plurality of affected groups. If this assertion be valid, it follows that any grand social accounting for a 'whole community' is meaningless, for it hides the distribution of costs and benefits among the affected groups. I suggest that, until we can make group-specific evaluations about the distribution of goods and services among the various communities, we are bound to neglect just those community-value consequences that matter most.

In recent years a number of sophisticated efforts have been made to trace the magnitudes of costs and benefits that would be generated by proposed governmental actions. These aggregative studies (still the prototype in this field) are inherently oblivious to community pluralism. They are used to justify projects whose overall benefits may well exceed their overall costs all right, but which nonetheless may impose considerable hardships upon some persons. Such studies, therefore, may prove to be more harmful than useful. A few studies, seeking to trace the incidences of costs and benefits, are more promising for they seek to anticipate which persons will be helped and which hurt.

But, even if we could accurately forecast the likely distributions of external costs and benefits to specific groups or communities and compare the consequences of alternative courses of action, how are public decisions then to be made? How are we to know what distribution of benefits and costs would be best? Here our technical analytical heritage fails us; it provides no basis for determining how benefits *should* be distributed. As Princeton economist William Baumol has put it: 'There is nothing in economic analysis which permits us to say that individual A should optimally receive [a fixed amount of income or other benefit more than] B. The value judgements involved in recommending a distribution of income must somehow be grafted onto the economic information . . .'[10] Because economic theory has nothing to say about the comparative advantages of alternative distributions, we have always dealt with these questions politically. By now there are many overt governmental practices that are explicitly intended to redistribute incidences of benefits and costs. Unashamedly, they are politically determined. Elderly persons who could not possibly benefit from public education of the young are nonetheless required to pay the taxes that support state schools. Welfare payments to the poor are distributed from general tax revenues. Housing is supplied with governmental funds at low rents that are commensurate with low incomes. In the United States, federal grants for public transit service are now having to pass a new kind of test, a political test, after they have passed their technical tests. The new question is: what will the proposed transit project do for the poor?

However novel the redistributional criteria may be for transportation engineers, they are old ones to city planners. And yet, by having adopted the engineer's idea of *standards*, the distributional objectives are inevitably short-circuited.

55

Standards [11]

These standards establish minimum permissible qualities for goods and services. These are distinct from those other kinds of standards that set units of measurement (for example, the gramme, centimetre, second), or that are used in industry to permit interchangeability of parts (the configuration of screw threads, for example), or that refer to current experiential norms (as with 'standards of living' or 'academic standards').

Behind the conception of administered or legislated quality standards is the more fundamental idea of *requirements*. The source is clear, for the idea has been developed to its most refined stage in the various fields of engineering. If a given span is to be bridged, a beam of specifiable dimensions is required. If a given amount of water is to be transported at a specified pressure, a pipe of determinate dimensions is required. Behind these determinations lies a body of theory in physics and an accumulated body of empirical tests and experimental findings. Each of these statements is also explicit about the *goals* to be served: if your goal is to span that river, do this; if your goal is to carry water, do that. Having a firm scientific and empirical base and an explicit statement of objectives, engineers have been able to write standards that conform to those *conditional* requirements. Their approach was adopted at an early stage by practitioners in public health. In turn, it became standard-operating-procedure in city planning.

But when the requirements-and-standards approach was transplanted into the city planning field, neither the scientific basis nor the explicit goals was attached. Lacking an accumulated body of scientific inquiry in the urban field, we have had little hard evidence on which we could rely. Faced with a multiplicity of communities, each with its own goal systems, how was one to know which standards were appropriate?

The problem was solved by dropping the engineer's *conditional* qualification. The 'if' clause was eliminated, and requirements became the expression of what are called 'needs'. As best I understand the idea, needs are seen as absolute necessities, not as conditional preferences. Of course, no prices are attached because no *comparison* of values is possible, nor are trade-offs among competing 'requirements' and 'needs' possible. As *absolute* necessities, they are all equally, and infinitely, valued ends.

In this manner the economizing basis for selecting standards and for selecting courses of action was rejected in favour of ideologically derived assertions of imperatives. In this fashion, too, markets were cut out as indicators of value. Consumers' own market statements about their mix of preferences were replaced by externally adjudged assertions about their needs. Lacking causal theory that might have permitted one to say 'if a given group wants A, they need to do B', professional judgments were substituted for both A and B. Lacking knowledge of separate groups' wants, professionals decreed the conditions of a universal public welfare. The effect was inevitably thereby to neglect the wants of some publics. The tactic has been so successful that it is by now widespread among the social professions.

Thus, educators proclaim what is good for children, Because they usually do know more than others about education, they have been able to make the operational decisions. Medical people are surely among the most powerful of the professionals; each of us confidently puts his life in his physician's hands, on the presumption that he knows what is best. And so, too, with a growing array of professionals from television repairmen to solicitors.

As the professions have been able to claim expertise and, thus, popular deference, they have taken over control of the various agencies in which they work. Medical people effectively control the governmental medical services, recreationists the park departments, engineers the public-works agencies, and so on. Each field is guided by its own ideology—by profession-specific notions of individuals' 'needs'. Each also has its own altruistic perceptions of the 'public welfare', which typically relies, of course, upon the very sorts of services that the given profession offers.

With his characteristic perceptive acuity, George Bernard Shaw put it most sharply in reporting that 'each profession is a conspiracy against the laity'. His judgment has since been supported by the findings of investigators more systematic than he, who have recently been studying the bureaucratic processes and delivery systems of the social services. Their research is revealing that the lay groups least served are those who enjoy less-than-middle-class status and who have the least developed skills for dealing with professional suppliers. Among the sharpest of these examinations that I have seen are those by Martin Meyerson [12] and by Martin Rein.[13] Meyerson notes that American social policy has been directed toward servicing the 'center-based majorities', perhaps a necessary consequence of supplying standardized services that conform to the preferences of the greatest number of consumers. But the further consequence is that the multifarious minority groups are not well served. In a field he studied intensely over the years, Meyerson is led to a discouraging conclusion: '. . . Urban housing policy of the federal government

57

had as a major aim the improvement of the position of the low-income consumer of housing. Instead, if it strengthened the position of the consumer of housing at all, it was the middle-income household which benefited. Furthermore, most of the gains accrued to the builders and the mortgage lenders. As for urban renewal, it has often replaced the poor in favor of the rich'.[14]

Similar patterns have emerged in other social services—in law, education, transportation, police protection—even (where one might least expect it) in the 'war on poverty'. The accumulating evidence supports the most cynical view: that the social professions have been in the business of serving themselves rather than their clients. The professions' orientation to efficiency on the supply side, to the neglect of equity on the demand side of the system, have surely fostered that sort of producer bias. But no conspiratorial motivations nor racial or class prejudice need be read into it. I believe the cause is simply that professionals have been wearing cultural blinders that narrow their peripheral vision. The middle-class professionals have been unable to understand that some people just do not want what middle-class people may want. They find it difficult to communicate with lower-class clients. They have had no empirical output measures of consumer satisfaction, and so they have sought to improve the lot of the relatively deprived by supplying the mix of services and facilities preferred by middle-class consumers. These, at least, have the authoritative majority stamp of adequacy.

Cultural barriers to communication are difficult to cross. That is why psychiatrists, for instance, have found it so hard to treat lower-class patients. The valuational, behavioural, and social organizational differences between their cultures are so wide that they cannot be fully understood by psychiatrists. Teachers are faced with the same problem. So are physicians, nurses, social workers, city planners, and policemen. And so, in turn, are the agencies these professions control. The professional shares the behavioural and value norms of middle-class culture, and middle-class culture is simply different from the non-middle-class cultures of other groups. As Oscar Lewis has been at pains to explain, what he calls 'the culture of poverty' is indeed a different social system. The working-class and lower-class publics, who have inadequate social skills for dealing with the majority culture, thus have difficulty in breaking through the cultural barriers that surround hospitals, schools, housing administrations, and the like. When income deficiencies further reduce their capacities for breaking into the markets, their handicap in accomplishing their own purposes is compounded.

58

In casting this account in the simplistic language of two or three social classes, I recognize that it cartoons an extraordinarily complicated network of publics. The rapidly increasing pluralism of publics, reflecting the rising affluence of the late-industrial and the early post-industrial periods, may spell the demise of whatever beginnings of a 'mass' society we might once have had. Indeed, it is this growing pluralism that impels me to question the contemporary precepts of professional practice. If the social professions, including city planners, are to hold to their concepts of 'needs', 'requirements' and 'standards'; if they are to continue to seek standardized solutions to problems and standardized objectives for change; if the coming rise of planning should mean further centralization of authority and power in the hands of professional governmental officials—then our style of practice might not permit us to serve the very aims we professionals profess.

SOME PROSPECTS FOR REDIRECTION

At the outset I described planning as a rational approach to accomplishing explicit purposes, and governmental planning as fundamentally oriented to the welfare pay-offs redounding to the various publics' separate purposes. I suggested that the only acceptable test of a governmental programme is an appraisal of how well-off the various client-groups become as a result. The meaningful test of effectiveness can be applied only on the output side, never on the input side.

If there is a single rule of systems analysis and of economics, if there is a single relevant canon of science, this is it: the only acceptable test of an hypothesis—including a policy or an action hypothesis—is whether it works when you try it out. The measure we must meet is demonstrated-effectiveness of outcomes—effectiveness as measured against explicitly enunciated goals. One of the long-standing habits of the traditional social professions has been to measure worth on the input side. Standards are input criteria. So are land-use and building regulations. So are teacher-student ratios and doctor-patient ratios. So are numbers of hospital beds, school buildings, highways, and the rest of the facilities governments build. And so, too, are monetary and fiscal policies and virtually all governmental programmes.

To be sure, all these constraints and facilities are intended to accomplish certain purposes. They have seldom been overtly considered to be ends in themselves. And yet, because these purposes are so seldom made explicit, and because these means have

59

become the stocks of the trades, it is difficult to avoid the inference that the aim of the professions has been to apply the professional instruments.

The give-away comes when one tries to find out whether they *do* serve intended purposes. The evidence is typically nowhere to be found. Despite the gigantic investments in new towns in Britain, for example, no one has yet attempted to find out whether new town residents are any better off than anyone else. Despite the elaborate epidemiological apparatus, we still do not know whether public health and medical services are making people healthier; we know only about rates of illness. No one has attempted to find out whether American land-use zoning has accomplished its purposes—whatever those purposes might be.

There is no evidence because we have not been explicit or specific about our aims for specific publics and because we rarely go back to evaluate what happened. I know of no studies by city planning agencies to appraise the welfare returns to their client groups. Were it not that a few sociologists have been curious, we would have little notion of what it means to live in the Bethnal Greens, the Belfasts, the Levittowns, or the Harlems of this world. City planning measures its success on the input side. We test our productivity by asking how large our staffs and our budgets are, how many cases were processed, how many houses were built, how many miles of highway, how many acres of parks. We do not ask how well-off are the people who live in the houses, use the highways, or play in the parks. We do not ask about the various consumers' schedules of preferences—about the mix of public commodities and services of various quality they desire as they weigh their wants against the spectra of attached prices.

Charles Lindblom contends that, whenever we do enunciate ends, we 'select them to conform to the available means'.[15] Further, it looks as though our ends have become, *per se*, the sheer application of the available means. Despite the high purposes we proclaim, we seem to live for the professional game. Our pay-offs come from playing the game well, as judged by our professional peers who distribute the rewards that matter most to us. We have no other tangible evidence of success, for we have no external measures of the welfare returns to our client publics.

I expect this picture will be changing swiftly, however. Current work in benefit-cost analysis and cost-effectiveness analysis, the newly emerging social indicators, and the move toward programme-budgeting are now all converging and may soon trigger an output- and client-orientation in the city planning field. The change is already underway in America. But even if we abandon the engineer's thoughtways and internalize the economist's valuational thoughtways, we shall still face the distributional questions that growing pluralism, rising affluence, and persisting poverty will force upon us.

Baumol and his colleagues tell us that economic theory can be of little help in resolving the equity questions. We are, therefore, left with a cluster of political questions that no technical methods can mask. It does not matter that politicians, publics and planners prefer to believe otherwise and commonly mask these questions and their decisions as being 'merely technical' ones. The equity side of every planning coin is political on its face. Planning is unavoidably and inherently a political activity. I mean that the decisions taken on such important matters as sewage systems, housing, transport, schools and airports are *political decisions*. No matter how competent the supporting scientific analyses, or how sophisticated the simulation models, these techniques can test only efficiency and, at best, only identify distributional consequences. Insofar as the outcomes of planned actions effect a reallocation of benefits and costs (and they almost always do), the problems they address can have no technical solutions—only political ones.

In a democratic society the interplay of partisan groups effectively determines not only what is *wanted*, but therefore, what is *right*. After the technical criteria have been met, the residual (and often determining) evidence is the preferential statements by consumers and by externally affected groups. Open political debate has always been a way of finding equitable outcomes—in part because competing wants can thus be weighed in the political balance, in part because competing wants can then be adjudicated. But public debate is an operational mode also because political expression of preferences is the only way we have to assess appropriate distributions of benefits and costs.

Market places are the counterpart of political forums—the media through which individual purchasers express their preferences as well as the relative weightings they assign to their competing preferences. There are indeed conditions that markets cannot deal with. But there are also many public enterprises, which at present make no direct charge for their services to consumers, whose services could be priced. We do charge for some governmentally provided services (for example, postal, public housing) and we could use the pricing system for other services as well. As yet we have no better way to find out what consumers want than by observing their behaviour under conditions of wide choice. Whether we are considering art museums or automobiles, the political forum and the market place together provide the sensitive testing instruments (on the output

61

side of the systems) for determining the amounts, types and qualities of public goods or private goods that *should* be supplied.

This is all very well for the wealthy, of course, but persons with but little money have little effective choice in the market place; persons with but little power have little effective voice in the political arena. This is generally true. But, the issue of income distribution among social groups is a separable question from the issue of appropriate mix of public goods and services, and it must be attacked frontally. Yet, given the current facts about income distribution and about costs attached to the available goods and services, our first question must ask how each person chooses to allocate his income among his various wants. However imperfect, such expressions are likely to be more accurate indicators of goodness than are professional divinations. The professions' problem of determining how much of what kinds of public goods and services to supply could be solved in part by adopting quasi-market processes that will supply feedback about wants from consumer to supplier.

I am suggesting that we attach prices to many governmental services that are now distributed without charge. The aim is not, of course, to return to the laissez-faire traditions of the past. Rather, it is to build into our decision-and-action processes those feedback loops which are essential to accomplishing the welfare objectives we seek. Only if each group has a tap into those loops so that it can express its special wants will we be able to serve the growing numbers of minorities and help those who most need help. The requirements-and-standards approach we have institutionalized is intrinsically insensitive to cultural pluralism. Inherently orientated to the middle of the middle-class, it has worked to the inevitable disadvantage of already disadvantaged groups.

In effect, I am suggesting that the social professions made a mistake somewhere along their historical paths. By substituting profession-specific criteria for markets and political forums, they thought they were removing the problems posed by market imperfections. Instead they created an additional devilish hurdle for consumers. It is not even clear whether American lower-class consumers and other minority groups are any better off for these efforts.

The Validity and Variety of Planned Interventions

As I have already indicated, there are indeed varieties of goods and services that private markets cannot deal with. They cannot handle externalities; private suppliers cannot provide purely public goods; private investors cannot undertake large, high-risk investments; and so on. Certainly all regulations cannot be eliminated. Certainly governmental enterprise will become increasingly necessary.

But even with clear instances of market incapacities (such as the blatant social costs of the river-pollution variety) harmful behaviour might best be constrained by applying incentives rather than direct prohibitions. The voluntary association of Ruhr Valley manufacturers has turned a polluted river into a fresh water supply; the income-tax incentives in America and elsewhere have induced builders to supply needed types of housing; and examples of other successful inducements are now becoming numerous. External social benefits probably cannot be dealt with except through taxation. I, for one, am quite prepared to accept the superiority of governmental information regarding harmful products; the restrictions on drugs, for example, are clear instances in which constraints on individual choice are warranted. But it is equally evident that such constraints must themselves be imposed with severe constraint, lest individuals' prerogatives be usurped by well-meaning moral policemen.

The most difficult questions attach to prohibitions on individual free choice in the name of short-run public benefits (the ninth rationale). Controls of this sort are popular among city planners such as those applying to the use of automobiles and the holding of private land in undeveloped state; among other professionals are various controls on behaviour intended to protect the moral order. I can find no justification for elitist constraints of these kinds; I can see only the erosion of personal freedom at the end of the path. Again, if we could indeed predict confidently that shifts in behaviour would lead to improvements in well-being, it would be far better to devise incentive schemes that encourage individuals rather than to apply the crude administrative regulations to which we have become addicted.

But then, suppose we were clever enough to invent ways of supplying differentiated public goods and services and to price them as a test of consumer wants; suppose we were innovative enough to invent incentive systems which could supplant standards and regulation. These measures alone would not result in satisfied consumers if their purchasing power were low. We would also have to effect a redistribution of incomes so that those who are now poor could acquire the operational capacity for choice and, most important, so that their children could break away from the generational cycle that now turns working-class children into working-class adults.

At an earlier period of history, direct payments to low-income earners and selective distribution of services carried the very sorts of personal degradation that Richard Titmuss has been cautioning us

63

about. In America the welfare system has been so overlaid by social workers' policing activities that 'welfare' has come to mean its antonym. To avoid the symbolic meanings attached to the dole, designers of social service programmes sought to distribute services directly and universally, in the manner of the British National Health Service. But that route carries all the overburden of problems I have been outlining.

Perhaps we are now prepared to accept a minimum level of income as a right, as the British public has come to accept health services. Several methods for redistributing income are now being explored. The negative-income-tax is especially promising, for it would meet many of the problems mentioned above. By creating conditions of effective consumer choice, it might thereby reduce the roles of professionals in making decisions for consumers. Once it gained favour across the entire political spectrum, the negative-income-tax (or some equally automatic way of establishing an income floor) could soon become a new basis for distributing services. If sufficiently high minimum-income levels can be maintained, we could employ market-type distribution systems to expand the range of choice open to minority consumer groups. Even were all families suddenly to become wealthy, the problems of governmental planning would not disappear, of course, but many problems associated with supplying governmental services and facilities would be removed.

SUMMARY

The post-industrial age will be marked by increasingly diverse publics having increasingly diverse wants and being increasingly involved in political affairs. The combination of diversity with political participation will engender vocal demands for widening arrays of services and facilities. Compound interest rates working on small minorities will inevitably turn them into large minorities, increasingly able, politically, to claim those services. Standards and standardized regulations are not the media that match diversity of wants. Instead, where effective markets do not exist to monitor shifting wants and to feed information back into the planning system, we shall need to invent surrogate market systems to guide public planning.

The burden of my argument is that city planning failed to adopt the planning method, choosing instead to impose input bundles, including regulatory constraints, on the basis of ideologically defined images of goodness. I am urging, as an alternative, that city planning tries out the planning idea and the planning method.

During the next decades, planning is likely to become the normal mode of deciding and acting in a wide array of societal affairs. At the same time, we shall be living with increasing affluence, increasing relative poverty, and increasing power in the hands of the few technically proficient planners. It will then be all the more necessary that decisions be guided by the *outputs* of government actions, outputs measured by their welfare benefits to the plurality of publics who will inhabit the post-industrial society. The concepts and methods that emerged during the early days of the industrial age are not likely to suit us in the post-industrial age. Now, and increasingly in the future, the hard decisions will have to rely upon explicit statements of the wants of the publics.

Who, then, is to pay and who is to profit? Only the political process can give us these answers. If we do not agree with the outcomes, we still hold the option of using our growing professional influence to effect the political balance. As I have been contending, planning is inside the political system, and, hence a growing political force in itself. I would wish it to use its growing power toward assuring that the goods, services, and facilities supplied are sufficiently diverse to satisfy even the smallest minority's wants. That is to say, a central principle for public planning is that we use the instruments of government in promoting a diversity of goods and services that the market processes have been failing to deliver.

Who is to decide? Clearly, a wide array of competing groups in and out of government. But if the planning idea can be made to work, an increasing proportion of decisions must be made by individual consumers. After all, they are the ones who know what they want. Far more frequently than we permit ourselves to think, they are also the only ones who know what is best for them.

The post-industrial age will bring unprecedented affluence to Western societies. It will also make possible, for the first time in history, a range of choice sufficient to satisfy the preferences of all groups in those societies. The planning idea would accelerate that development. As the counterpart of the idea of democracy, and as an instrument for promoting freedom, I suggest it is worth our giving it a try.

References

1. Z. Brzezinski, 'America in the Technetronic Era', *Encounter*, January 1968, pp. 16–17.

2. D. N. Michael, *Cybernation: The Silent Conquest*, Centre for the Study of Democratic Institutions, Santa Barbara, 1962.

3. M. G. Salvadori speaking on 'The Impact of Science and Technology' at a private conference, 1964.

4. D. Bogue, 'The End of the Population Explosion', *The Public Interest*, No. 7, Spring 1967, pp. 11–201.

5. R. L. Meier, *Studies on the Future of Cities in Asia*, Centre for Planning and Development Research, University of California, 1967.

6. K. Davis, 'Urbanization in India', *India's Urban Future*, R. Turner (Ed.), University of California Press, 1962, p. 25.

7. B. Harris, *Inventing the Future City*, Catherine Bauer Wurster Memorial Lecture, University of California, Berkeley, 1966 (mimeographed).

8. Herbert Gans has summarized with insight the ideology of the American city planning movement, 'City Planning in America: A Sociological Analysis', in *International Encyclopedia of the Social Sciences*, Free Press, Macmillan, 1968, pp. 129–37.

9. R. Dorfman, *Measuring Benefits of Government Investments*, Brookings Institution, 1965, p. 8.

10. W. J. Baumol, *Economic Theory and Operations Analysis*, Prentice-Hall, 2nd edition, 1965, p. 356.

11. The section on standards owes much to John W. Dyckman.

12. M. Meyerson, 'National Urban Policy Appropriate to the American Pattern', in *Goals for Urban America*, B. J. Berry and J. Meltzer (Eds), Spectrum Books, Prentice-Hall, 1967.

13. M. Rein, 'The Social Crisis', *Transactions*, May 1964, pp. 3–6, 31–32.

14. M. Meyerson, op. cit., p. 74.

15. A. O. Hirschman and C. E. Lindblom, 'Economic Development, Research and Development, Policy Making: Some Converging Views', *Behavioural Science*, Vol. VII, No. 2, April 1962, pp. 215–16.

Chapter 2

Beyond the Inter-disciplinary Approach to Planning

WILLIAM ALONSO

Because the problems that confront the city and regional planner seldom respect the boundaries of traditional academic disciplines, it is often suggested that an inter-disciplinary collaboration is needed to incorporate the techniques, knowledge, and peculiar viewpoints of several disciplines. Among the most commonly mentioned specialties are architecture, engineering, sociology, psychology, economics, and political science.

In the early 1950s, when I started studying architecture and planning at Harvard, the influence of Walter Gropius was preeminent and the ideal of inter-disciplinary collaboration was a keystone to broadening the design professions to include most particularly the social sciences. Since then, I have been part of many inter-disciplinary teams and have participated in many discussions of this subject. I now think that the inter-disciplinary approach is of limited validity and that the apparent common sense of this approach hides many pitfalls. It is necessary to look at the concrete problems to be attacked, at the potential contribution of the collaborating professions, and at the specific ways in which these elements mix. Because the case for the inter-disciplinary approach is well-known and its virtues generally accepted, I shall concentrate on the case against it.

THE INTER-DISCIPLINARY RECIPE

The ordinary recipe for the inter-disciplinary approach goes something like this: 'Take a physical planner, a sociologist, an economist; beat the mixture until it blends; pour and spread.' Whether political scientists, psychologists, traffic engineers, philosophers, artists, architects, or zoologists are included seems to depend on the availability of people, the limitations of the budget, and the imagination of those assembling the team. What is wrong with this? Any problem in urban or regional planning, except the most trivial, involves physical design, social aspects, economic aspects, political aspects, ecological aspects, and the like. What is more sensible than to say,

'Let us then get an expert in each of these fields, have the experts meet, present their special viewpoints and competences, weigh the pros and cons as reasonable men, and as a body arrive at recommendations which are informed by each of the contributing disciplines on each of the component problems?'

Consider, for instance, the proposition of taking an economist. An economist is a person who has a degree in economics. He may be an institutional economist, reared in discursive treatments of selected subjects in a style close to that of sociology or political science. Or he may be a fairly abstract type, whose principal background consists of proving the convexity of sets or existence theorems. Or he may be an econometrician, skilled in the interpretation of beta coefficients as measures of elasticity and in dealing with the particular difficulties of serial autocorrelation in time series. Or he may be a monetary theorist, or a welfare economist, or an economic historian, or any of a hundred other specialties within the discipline. The problem at hand may call for the particular expertise of cost-benefit, but 'the economist' may be a location theorist. Or the problems may involve analyses of regional economies, and this man's strength may be the applications of game theory. There is no need to drive the point further. Economics, like every other discipline, has become a conglomerate of diverse specialties, and any one member of the profession is guaranteed to be utterly ignorant of most branches outside his own specialty. It would be almost by coincidence that the particular economist drafted for the task happened to be expert in the particular areas needed, unless he were drafted by someone informed in the varieties of economics, familiar with the candidate's competence, and able to anticipate the particular specialties that would be needed.

There is a further difficulty in 'taking an economist' which is seldom mentioned because it is touchy. An economist (and I am still using an economist only as an example) is a member of a learned profession within which the rewards go to those who are held in high esteem by other members of that same profession. Thus, it does an economist no good to be regarded highly by artists or sociologists. This will not get him promotion in a university or any other form of recognition. In an applied case tackled by an inter-disciplinary team, the needs of the situation will demand from the economist rough-and-ready solutions to dimly perceived problems. If these solutions happen to be noticed by his peers (which is unlikely), they are far likelier to bring forth criticism of their shortcomings rather than praise for their ingenuity. In an academic situation, where an economist teaches in an inter-disciplinary programme, the time he needs to inform himself in other areas will limit his ability to keep current in his own field. Further, his teaching is likely to consist principally of repetitions of introductory material, which is often misunderstood by students whose interests lie elsewhere, and he will lack the challenge and stimulation of having advanced students in his own field, whose work keeps him at the top of his form and whose research serves as an extension of himself.

Under these circumstances, it has been common for the 'economist' to be one of three types: 1. A man who is not very good, therefore not much in demand, and thus available. He may be skilled in one technique or another, but on the whole he will not have the inventiveness, flexibility, and range of mind to do other than repeat what he has learned and done before. He will not so much collaborate as add himself. 2. An older, distinguished member of the profession, whose position is secure, but who is now slightly bored with the narrowness of discipline, and who is perhaps having difficulties in keeping up with the more technical work of his younger colleagues. Such men can contribute brilliant insights, but they are often tempted into playing the role of the great man, given to philosophizing, contributing more as wise man than as expert. 3. A professional or individual eccentric, who may reject the traditional avenues of advancement in his profession or whose ideas may be so unusual that these avenues are closed to him. Such individuals may be extraordinarily creative and valuable, but they are mutants in the evolution of their field, and rarely are mutations successful.

Thus, there is a double fallacy in the concept of getting 'an economist' for the collaborative team. The first fallacy is that the label 'economist' is a standard product that can deliver upon demand the viewpoint of his discipline on any given subject. The second is that the institutional sociology of the professional team makes it extremely likely that 'the economist' shall be a mediocrity, a seniority, or an eccentric. There are relatively few men who are mature, on top of their field, productive, flexible, and fully capable of participating as 'the economist,' and there are so many demands upon their time and talents that an ad hoc inter-disciplinary effort is unlikely to appeal to them.

Aside from problems of availability and suitability of participants, collaborative teams face other difficulties. I will mention only two, one of them mechanical, the other more fundamental. The mechanical problem is a version of Parkinson's Law that work expands to fill the time available. Except in the largest and most long-lived teams, the number of representatives from each discipline will be determined by budget, availability, and what economists call the indivisibility of inputs. The basic team consists of equal fractions of one representative from each field, but the project may call for more work by one discipline and less by the others. The consequence of this is that one man is overworked and others are underworked. The underworked team members may well create useless activities to fill out the time, or they may lose interest and stop attending. Clearly, this is inefficient—the overworked discipline should be given more resources and the underworked less. A common variant of this problem involves the staging of uneven work loads, because over the life of the project the effort demanded from each contributor will vary. The most frequent version of this problem concerns the interaction of physical designers and social scientists. Let us say that a new town is to be built. A team made up of an architect, an economist, and a sociologist is assembled. The economist and the sociologist go off to find data on which to base their recommendations, and they may not have anything useful to say to the architect until months later. The architect, meanwhile, is left alone with pencil and paper, and he will naturally start making designs for the new town. By the time the economist and the sociologist return, they may find that the architect has completed a design and that their recommendations will be resented by him if they threaten to change the design. The consequence in this case is not a mere waste of inputs, but a distortion of the resulting plan. Inter-disciplinary collaboration may become inter-disciplinary conflict without well-managed staging of the operation.

The other problem is a more fundamental one. The team brings together members of different intellectual species, and some of these species rarely mix. They will use words differently, attribute different importance to various aspects, and hold different views of their own and others' competencies and interests. The architect may view the economist as a fancy engineering cost estimator and as a philistine interested only in efficiency. The economist may think that the concern of the sociologists for power and non-market social organization is not useful and that the market will take care of things. The sociologist may be mystified by the social philosophy of the architect. Words like 'marginal', 'rational', 'dynamic', 'group', will have different meanings for each of them, and will probably lead to confusion. With time, tolerance, and patience, they will come to understand each other better, but great areas of each discipline have logical and symbolic foundations which cannot, except imperfectly and through extraordinary effort, be melded with other disciplines. The difficulty in mixing approaches is illustrated in my experience in teaching the social sciences to urban designers. Many of them became reasonably good social scientists, but when they began to design, they usually shed the social science approach and reverted to traditional approaches to design. They would call singly on either training but not on both at the same time. Only a very few students were able to combine these two intellectual skills, and then only self-consciously and in limited ways. The fundamental differences among disciplines explain why so many inter-disciplinary team reports are not true collaborations but collections of chapters individually authored.

THE ALTERNATIVE: AN URBAN AND REGIONAL DISCIPLINE

As a positive alternative to the inter-disciplinary concept, I advocate that urban and regional problems and plans be attacked by one or more professionals who are first and foremost scholars in urban and regional problems and secondarily members of traditional disciplines. This is quite different from the concept of inter-disciplinary collaboration which implies bringing together people who are primarily economists or sociologists and who, whatever their standings in their primary professions, tend to be amateurs in the field of urban and regional problems. Let me make clear that in calling for urban experts I am not falling into the Leonardo da Vinci trap, which is assembling an endless inventory of compartments of human knowledge and calling on planning students to master it. Obviously, no one person can, and many of the items in the inventory cannot be taught because nobody knows how.[1] Instead, I will suggest that competent specialists in the socio-economic aspects of urban and regional development already exist and that the job is to train more of these people rather than to invent them.

William James suggested that there were two varieties of social science: the hard and the soft. Cohesive urban specialties have developed within each of these two varieties as the result of years of sustained scholarly interest and communication in the substantive issues of urban and regional development. This substantive focus serves to reduce the importance of disciplinary distinctions. However, there is still a considerable gap between the soft and the hard varieties.

The hard social sciences are those that measure with precision, combine their numbers into fairly complexly articulated models, seek reproducible results, and in general behave much like the natural sciences. The soft social sciences, on the other hand, deal more in words, in insights, and often concern themselves with qualitative differences and dialectical situations which do not easily lend themselves to mathematical treatments. They often stress creativity and originality rather than reproducibility. To illustrate, it is fairly clear

71

that the mathematical models that normally appear in the pages of Regional Science publications belong to the hard school, and that the current writings on the political aspects of the racial situation in the United States belong mostly to the soft.[2]

Within the hard social sciences, there has emerged in just a few years a common ground among people from many parent disciplines. Thus, every year several hundred scholars gather at the Regional Science Association Conference and present and discuss papers. The participants may be economists, geographers, planners, political scientists, sociologists, systems analysts, and the like, but at these meetings they present and receive papers which share a defined range of topics, a body of techniques, and certain standards of validation. They share, to a large degree, a technical language and competence, and they read much of the same literature. These meetings are not inter-disciplinary, but rather meta-disciplinary, since the participants gather together not because of their diversity but because of their commonality.

Further, within the hard urban and regional social sciences, the range of subjects and techniques, though evolving and growing, is a well defined set and can be taught. There are concise and clear texts by which students may be trained in these subjects, without having to go back to first statements in the technical journals or into arcane intricacies. Today a department interested in urban studies may, by requiring from good students one to three years of effort, train them to the point where they will know well one or two areas and be at least familiar with the remainder of the subjects. Whether the products of such training are to be called economists, geographers, systems planners, or regional scientists, they will bring to any particular situation a better sense of which problems can be tackled profitably and which cannot, and they will be versed in the relevant techniques and experience.

The situation is less clear in the case of the soft social sciences, such as sociology, political science, and psychology. Certain elements of these soft sciences are quite hard. For instance, sociologists or psychologists have techniques of surveying populations, statistical inference, and demographic analysis, while political scientists have some very concrete knowledge of governmental processes. I am calling them soft to characterize their concern with and competence in subjects in which judgment and opinion play a very large role.

Because the techniques are not well established, it seems to me that the soft social scientist has little to contribute to a team *unless* his judgment is informed by experience and by knowledge of most of the relevant substantive literature on the particular issues. This literature goes considerably beyond that defined by the academic peer group as being within the discipline. Indeed, many of the most significant advances are made outside conventional academic circles, and the academic establishment lags in its recognition of these issues. The people who know most about the social aspects may be sociologists or political scientists, but they may also be lawyers, architects, or almost anything else, provided that they have been keenly interested in the subject for a number of years and have read, observed, and thought about it as much as they could. Without this background, the soft scientist on an inter-disciplinary team tends to react in a negative way by finding fault with the discussions of others, to escape into matters of detail, or to become giddy with millenary visions. This is, in part, because sociology has been most successful at explaining the functionality of existing patterns but has been much less successful at projecting change. Sociologists are still concerned with establishing the credentials of their discipline as a science, and they follow the scientific procedure of doubting and testing any proposition before accepting it. But in planning work, where it is necessary to make recommendations and decisions and where things must be said even when certainty does not exist, it is necessary to develop ways of dealing reasonably with uncertainty. Whereas the hard social sciences have developed fairly useful methods of doing this, the soft ones have not. Applied work dealing with the future is an exercise in the art of risk-taking. Because their fields have not developed accepted styles for this activity, most soft social scientists cope with uncertainties and risk-taking with as much professionalism as a lady who has been taken to the horse races.

Nonetheless, there seems to be emerging a group of soft meta-disciplinary specialists who are knowledgeable about academic and non-academic literature, the problems of government, and the social realities and who have developed a sense of the possible and of the manner in which risks are taken.[3] However, there is not yet a sufficiently defined core of transmittable knowledge, with efficient texts and sustained mechanisms for association and communication among these social experts, for us to conceive of a manageable curriculum that would train a professional in this subject in a finite period of time.

My point, in brief, is that especially in the hard social sciences, but also in the soft ones, there has begun to develop a meta-disciplinary competence that rests in particular individuals, and that this provides a better model for the incorporation of the social sciences into the planning process than does the idea of an inter-disciplinary team. The key difference is that members of a meta-discipline share a common ground, while members of an inter-disciplinary team are brought together because of their diversity.

If my basic point is granted, the urgent need is to find a way to produce greater numbers of individuals with such competence to meet the demands of the work that must be done, as well as to do everything possible to advance these meta-disciplines. A meta-discipline cannot be called into immediate existence by an act of will. It requires patient and sustained rational effort, for there are few easy solutions, and development is slow and cumulative. It requires a great deal of money, and we must confer prestige and importance on this type of work to attract bright people to such careers.

The point of take-off seems to me to occur when there is a sufficient market in the field to support some division of labour between scientific and professional work. Scientific work advances knowledge by testing the limits of the known; thus, scientists are often willing to accept a high probability of failure in the expectation that the rare successes will be extremely valuable. Professional work applies a body of known theory and techniques to recurring situations. A powerful indicator of this take-off point is the emergence of a serious professional literature that expands the range of experience of the ordinary professional by reporting usefully and critically on the work of his fellow professionals, and which makes accessible to him the useful elements of recent scientific advances, stripped of unnecessary baggage, so that this material may be efficiently read and understood by everyone in the field.

NEW DEPARTURES

In a social system of significant size, most of the situations to which planning addresses itself have arisen before, or are very similar to other situations. The best and most efficient way of handling the vast majority of these cases is by repeating the logic and procedures of the most successful prior examples. Applying to this task an artistic criteria of creativity is irrelevant and invites a high rate of failure. It also wastes opportunities for the accumulation of knowledge. I would argue that most of planning is a professional exercise, in which the task is not to do something new but to do something well. In these circumstances, the professional's role is to identify the class of problem before him and to apply the best techniques known for solving that class of problem.

The situation is different where either the problem is unlike earlier problems or where previous solutions have been particularly poor. In that case, it is necessary to invent new approaches rather than to identify and apply existing ones. These circumstances call for a broader search and may justify bringing in ideas, minds and bodies of thought whose value is precisely that they differ from previous approaches. In such cases an inter-disciplinary team may be best. Nonetheless, it must be recognized that these occasions will be infrequent because the cost of serious research is very high, and the chances of success are very low. Further, there must be some basis for the belief that the case is in some way special. Otherwise the result may be that after much wasted motion the team re-invents the wheel. It would seem to me that on these unusual occasions, the team should be composed of urban specialists with a mixture of others who are specialists in various disciplines but who are not specialists on urban problems. Further, every effort should be made to insure that these other participants are of the intellectual calibre necessary for fundamental work, and that their available time and their dedication to the task are sufficient.

The preceding discussion has stressed examples from the social sciences rather than from the design disciplines. This reflects the shift of urban planning from its architectural origins and traditions toward the social sciences; this shift has accompanied the incorporation of planning and planners into the fabric of government and the weakening of the pattern of planning done by independent commissions or other groups. These developments have been good ones on the whole, making planning more effective and government more informed, but they have tended to weaken certain functions of the earlier style of planning which inter-disciplinary teams may sometimes perform.

The architectural origins of urban planning carried a tradition of structural radicalism, of holistic plans, and of professional ethics and integrity. Structural radicalism was highly valued, and plans were to be bold, innovative images of desirable futures. The tradition of holistic plans was reflected in the emphasis on master, comprehensive, or general plans. Although we would now view the agenda of these plans as too restricted, the planner was trying to paint a complete picture of the future, much as the architect draws a complete picture of the future building. The tradition of professional ethics and integrity held that the planner should advocate his convictions with as much vigour as possible. His plan might not be accepted, but he would not compromise.

The new style of planning is much more incremental, as shown by its reliance on such techniques as cost-benefit, PPBS, and programme

75

evaluation rather than on master plans. Its horizons are commonly tied to budgeting periods of one and five years rather than to the soaring twenty-five or fifty years of early plans. This incrementalism discourages consideration of radical structural changes. And because this planning is more closely tied to doing, in spite of taking into account many interrelations previously ignored, its prescriptions reflect the organization of government and deal with sectors rather than a holistic comprehensive plan. Finally, as planners have come to share the burden of operational responsibility, they have had to take into account viewpoints other than their own and interests different from their own interpretation of the public interest. They have become spokesmen and instruments of a collective process of decision. In gaining operational effectiveness, they have had to substitute societal ethics for professional ones, and they have lost the freedom to advocate their own convictions in the market place.

Although these developments represent a state of professional maturity, there are some losses. The sum of the parts of the incremental decisions may be either more or less than the whole. There may be interactions of individual decisions that are not anticipated, and decisions that are quite correct one at a time may lack decisiveness and direction, and thus fail. There is, then, a need for continuation of the architectural traditions in planning, by way of independent thinking, dissent, and long-range views. Radicalism and even utopianism are necessary to invent new alternatives, and even to invent new objectives. Long-range thinking, however uncertain and prone to error, is needed to see if the steps which we are taking one at a time lead us in the right direction. Holistic views are necessary to uncover relationships that are insufficiently recognized.

In the dialectic continuum between freedom and responsibility, traditional planning stood near the extreme of freedom, while the new developments look toward the extreme of responsibility. But urban and regional planning cannot afford to stand at either end of this continuum: it must occupy the full range, from individuals and institutions free to say what they wish (even if it is sometimes silly) to the centres of power, where responsible individuals may sometimes honourably follow policies with which they personally disagree. As planning in the old traditions becomes less frequent, the inter-disciplinary team, whose justification is the formulation of new departures, has a function as a possible source of innovation and dissent at the freedom end of the continuum. It is likely to find itself near the end of responsibility only in those cases where an eminent group is gathered to lend the legitimacy of their prestige to positions already taken by those who called them together.

Notes

1. In programmes of instruction based on this approach, it is all too common for individual members of the inter-disciplinary faculty to offer courses in their own specialties, with little or no idea of the contents of the rest of the curriculum. There are hopes that somehow the students will be able to synthesize all of this, but since mature scholars are unable to do so, it seems unlikely that students will succeed.

2. R. K. Merton has observed that there are two styles of sociology: the American (hard) and the European (soft). While the European is certain he is dealing with issues of fundamental importance, he has no way of knowing whether what he says is true. The American, dealing with quantitative materials, is quite certain that what he says is true, but he has no idea of what it means.

3. *Time* magazine has coined for them the unfortunate term 'urbanologists'.

Chapter 3

Observations on the Greater London Development Plan submitted to the Greater London Development Plan Inquiry by the Centre for Environmental Studies

DAVID DONNISON, with the assistance of
IRENE BREUGEL, MICHAEL HARLOE and DOREEN MASSEY.

I: INTRODUCTION

We are not objecting to the Plan but offering the Panel observations which may help them in their inquiry. Section II of this paper summarizes some of the main trends in the London housing market, and Section III comments on their human implications. Section IV shows that these implications pose a number of dilemmas for anyone adopting the aims expressed in the Development Plan, and Section V briefly outlines a pattern of policies for dealing with them. Although our analysis, thus far, is more explicit, more dogmatic and much less sophisticated than the GLC's, we do not think the Council would disagree greatly with it.

It is the sixth and seventh sections of the paper that constitute its point and purpose. In Section VI we argue that the action required to make a plan for Greater London effective must extend well beyond the powers and boundaries of the GLC, and the contents of a statutory Plan. The administrative, financial and political implications of the attempt to plan for Greater London have not been frankly discussed in the Plan, or by its critics. If the Panel were similarly constrained, their recommendations—and possibly the Minister's decision—would neglect the most important steps that must be taken to put the Plan into practice. Section VII points out the effects of these failings upon public participation in the planning process.

II: HOUSING

We follow the G.L.D.P. in starting from the supply of housing and considering some of the difficulties that arise from current trends in this market. Changes in supply will be concentrated mainly at, and

78

beyond, the borders of Greater London where the scope for new building is greatest, and in the inner parts of the town which will be fairly completely redeveloped or renewed in time. In these inner parts, built before the first world war, the following things are likely to happen.

The central core of administrative, commercial and cultural buildings, and the transport networks required to keep it working, will expand somewhat. This growth will be partly—perhaps wholly—offset by the closure of old industrial and commercial areas (markets and docks, for example) some of which will be rebuilt with housing.

The upper and middle income groups who live on the outer fringe and in sectors radiating northward and westward from the central core will extend their holdings in some places by acquiring previously rented housing for owner-occupation.

On a far bigger scale than either of these trends will be the replacement and (to a less extent) the improvement of older housing by local authorities.

All these trends will combine to hasten the disappearance of privately rented property: it constitutes most of the houses to be demolished and virtually none of those likely to be built. London will therefore suffer a massive loss of older, cheaper, smaller, rented dwellings, within easy reach of its central core. It will gain a lot of housing, mainly built for owner-occupiers and Council tenants. If past trends continue, most of these houses will be designed for young families. The new proposals announced by the Secretary of State* will bring welcome relief to poorer private tenants, but there is no reason to believe that they will reverse the trend of the past half century and enable the private landlord to become a major investor in new housing.

III: PEOPLE

One way of examining the effects of these changes is to ask who is likely to suffer from them. It is particularly difficult to generalize about the people who live in the sort of housing that is disappearing, for variety is their most striking characteristic. The following (frequently overlapping) groups are more heavily concentrated in London's older and poorer privately rented housing than elsewhere:

(a) old people with low incomes;
(b) single working people of all ages who want a small dwelling within easy reach of the centre;

* For rent allowances for private tenants.

(c) people entering the London labour and housing markets from their parents' homes in other parts of London, from the provinces or abroad, after service in the army or other professions, or in other ways. Most of these households are young, small and mobile; but some have several children or other dependants to support;

(d) temporary residents spending anything from a few weeks to a few years in London while training, doing business, or on leave from abroad;

(e) manual workers and their families, dependent on jobs which (owing to central location, shift-work, long hours, and low or insecure earnings) make it difficult for them to move to other kinds of housing.

Some of these people are very mobile and well able to look after themselves, others cannot find another home without help; most have small households, but some have very large ones; and many of them must be housed within inner London if the essential work now concentrated there is to be done. The disappearance of the housing on which they now rely does not squeeze out those best able to look after themselves. Nor are the most vulnerable families or the most essential workers all rehoused in the growing (public or owner-occupied) sectors of the housing market; many are already suffering severely from changes which are destined to go much further in the coming years.

IV: DILEMMAS

These trends and the problems they pose are common ground to the GLC and many of its critics. Although there is less agreement about solutions, the fundamental dilemmas to be resolved are widely recognized. They arise from the aims (also generally agreed) of plans for London's development. From the GLC's evidence to the Inquiry and its previous statements, the following aims emerge:

(a) to improve the whole quality of the environment throughout the crowded and more decayed parts of London;

(b) to improve the housing conditions of the worst-housed people;

(c) to ensure an adequate labour supply for the enterprises that are essential for London's economic health;

(d) to prevent a loss of the more highly skilled and paid people from London, the segregation of one social class from another, and the growing concentration of poorer people (or the richest and poorest) in London.

It is when these aims are brought together that dilemmas emerge. If the environment of inner London is to be improved, densities must be reduced and many people must move out; since it is the richer, the more skilled and the younger families who move out, their departure hastens tendencies to social segregation and polarization. The enterprises most characteristic of central London include service trades and small businesses paying low or widely fluctuating wages; such work does not enable people to pay the costs of better housing and a high quality environment, yet to move these workers out may destroy industries on which London's economy depends and leave people under-employed in suburbs and new towns where there are inadequate opportunities for the untrained. If the worst housed people are to be given overriding priority for subsidized Council housing in inner London, then others must be somehow compelled to leave this housing, the local authorities must reduce rents and may have to reduce building standards in order to house the poorest tenants, and massive social ghettos may be created in the process.

V: POLICIES

Clearly the aims of the Plan cannot be attained within the confines of the present locations of jobs, the present distribution of incomes, the present transport system, and present policies for housing, social security, taxation and subsidies. Either these patterns must be changed or some of the generally agreed goals must be jettisoned.

Outlined very briefly below is a pattern of policies that could attain these goals. They are not the best that could be devised; our purpose is only to show that any public authority intent on realizing goals of this sort must go a lot further than the GLC went (or was entitled to go?) in its Development Plans and seek commitments from all levels of Government over a wider range of questions than the Panel has so far been asked to consider.

These proposals are briefly summarized; they can be explained at much greater length if that would help the Panel.

(a) Lower paid and less skilled workers should be enabled to move out of central London to viable sub-centres in the outer Boroughs and beyond. That means that the industries employing them, their wives and children, should be moved to sites readily accessible from the homes of the less skilled.

(b) Public and private transport systems linking these sub-centres to the centre and to each other should be improved.

(c) The educational system, particularly in areas where schools are handicapped by social deprivations, should be deliberately

81

and selectively improved; the supply of unskilled workers must be reduced.

(d) Since public housing will shelter a growing proportion of the population, it should cater for a wider range of income groups and household types than is customary, and that means that rent levels, tenancy contracts and procedures of management must be reappraised.

(e) More privately rented housing should be acquired for public ownership, to keep it in the rented market, to put it into good condition while it remains in use, and to diversify the stock of housing available to local authorities.

(f) Rents in the public and private sectors of the market should be regulated and rationalized, so that they are comparable with each other and accord with the rent-paying capacities of the broad categories of households living in these sectors.

(g) A more generous system of family allowances or income supplements will be needed to assist larger families living on low wages.

(h) The remaining forms of housing subsidy and rate rebate should be redistributed to concentrate their help on those in greater need of it and to provide similar rights in all parts of London and in all sectors of the market. (The first subsidies to be reorganized should probably be the present tax reliefs on owner-occupiers' mortgage interest payments. Next, private tenants would be entitled to subsidies similar to those the Council tenant gets, to be administered by the same authorities.)

(i) More Council housing should be built in the outer Boroughs and beyond, related to job opportunities and transport systems which would enable some of the poorer families in inner London to move out.

(j) More housing for owner-occupation and for housing associations should be provided in some parts of the inner Boroughs where this would help to improve and retain older buildings or to diversify the social composition of the neighbourhood.

(k) To promote easier movement of less skilled workers from inner to outer Boroughs, and to new and expanded towns, special effort should be made, not only to rehouse and employ them, but to provide opportunities for education and training which will make them more skilled.

(l) Local housing authorities' debt burdens should be redistributed to enable all of them to play their part in the London housing programme.

This list of proposals could be extended, and each of them calls for a great deal of clarification and justification. But if it is agreed that policies broadly similar in scope are needed, the discussion can more fruitfully turn to the political, administrative and financial implications of such a programme.

VI: IMPLICATIONS

The most striking features of these proposals is that most of them do not fall within the responsibility of the GLC at all. Much of the road and the public transport systems are the Council's responsibility, and the schools of inner London are administered by the ILEA. But the Boroughs will build three-quarters of the Council housing that is to go up in Greater London: some are unwilling to collaborate with the GLC and others are financially unable to do so; each has its own priorities, its own policies and procedures for selecting tenants, for administering rent and rate rebates, and so on. Rights to nominate tenants to houses belonging to other authorities or to housing associations are a flimsy instrument of housing policy: nominees may be (and often are) assigned to the most unpopular houses, or they may be charged inadequately rebated rents which prevent them from accepting the tenancies offered. The location of new industry and offices depends mainly on the central government and the Boroughs. The location of passenger interchanges, car and lorry parks, the determination of densities, building standards and plot ratios, and even the regulation of taxis are all partly or wholly the responsibility of authorities other than the GLC. The number of people who move out of London, and the kind of people who go, will depend heavily on the growth of jobs and housing in new and expanded town schemes (and the distinction between the new and the expanded is an important one) and in other forms of overspill, planned and unplanned—few of which are directly controlled by the GLC.

The catalogue need not be extended: the GLC has made its weaknesses frankly clear to the Inquiry, and the Panel does not need to be told how British Government works. But if these basic features of our administrative system are not constantly borne in mind, it may too readily be assumed that the policies of the GLC, if approved by the Minister, will exert an influence on other authorities. That does not follow at all.

The G.L.D.P. lists the Action Areas already selected by Boroughs but does not comment on the fact that two of the Boroughs which have the most severe housing problems (Islington, and Kensington and Chelsea) have identified no such Areas. Can the GLC stir any Borough into action? Will it? The G.L.D.P. calls for more house building by private developers 'where appropriate', but does not say which areas would be most appropriate, or what action the GLC would take if this advice were only followed in the outer Boroughs to which it has appealed for more *Council* housing. Would it take any action at all? The Councils' officers, in opening statements to the Inquiry, said the Plan does not cover 'issues such as security of tenure or rent and rate rebates'. That may be inevitable, but the Plan cannot succeed unless action *is* taken on such issues. The Plan and the Inquiry have devoted a lot of time and paper to argument about population projections for London. Few have pointed out that these forecasts must depend on assumptions about the kinds of people who will live in London (the rich take up more space than the poor) and hence on the type, tenure and price of housing that is to be built in each Borough and the accessibility of these houses to jobs of various kinds. Thus a plan for (or a plan based on assumptions about) population must also be a plan for the evolution of housing, employment and transport, inside and outside London. Has the GLC worked out what part the Boroughs must play in such a plan? If so, who will ensure they play their part?

We hope the Panel will point out that its recommendations, whatever they may be, must extend well beyond the statutory content of the Plan and the broader questions so far considered at the Inquiry. This is partly an appeal for more power for the GLC; some of the Capital's problems would be easier to solve if the GLC were more clearly responsible for dealing with them. But the economic and social structure of London already extends so far beyond the Council's borders that no single local authority can be wholly responsible for meeting Londoners' needs. Much of the action required must be taken by the Central Government and by other authorities, local and regional. If it is not recognized that the policies eventually decided for the G.L.D.P. imply responsibilities for all levels of government, the aims of the Plan will soon be forgotten amidst the insoluble dilemmas of an authority that is powerless to attain them.

A heavy price will be paid in human and financial terms for this failure, but most of the bills will not be presented to those who prepared the Plan or appear at the Inquiry. In the education of Londoners a heavy price is already being paid for our failure to plan the development of their city more effectively. The educational options open to children from poorer and larger families begin to dwindle very early in life. The National Child Development Study has recently shown, yet again, that the school attainment of young children suffers from overcrowding and other pressures which are common in areas of low wages and housing shortage. Dr. Robson's recent study *Urban Analysis* (Cambridge University Press, 1969) shows, yet again, that rehousing in more spacious accommodation will not necessarily eliminate these handicaps: children's performance and their parents' aspirations for them depend partly on the social composition of their neighbourhood and the opportunities it affords. (Why stay a year longer at school unless you can get a better job by doing so? Why seek a better job unless you can get a better house with the extra money you earn?) The ILEA's study of sixth form opportunities in London shows that the reorganization they have so laboriously carried through to enlarge and equalize the opportunities of young people still leaves socially deprived areas with a poorer service than more fortunate areas. It is difficult to create a good sixth form in many parts of Tower Hamlets, Islington, Southwark and other places where academic talent, and teachers, are relatively scarce.

Education is only one of many fields in which the price of our failure to plan London's development is being paid. The ILEA's courageous policies for educational priority areas have been followed by community development projects, initiated by the Home Office, and an urban programme for which the Government has promised millions of pounds. Homeless families are now more generously treated than they used to be. Boarding-out allowances paid to foster parents have risen as high as the rent the foster-child's own mother may have been unable to pay. Plans are afoot for setting up publicly financed legal services in areas where no solicitors are to be found. The Government has recruited more police to handle London's special problems of law enforcement, and pays increasingly generous housing allowances and subsidies to enable these officers to find homes for their families in London.

Individually, each of these initiatives is splendid: we are building in the deprived areas of London a system of social services which foreigners travel long distances to study and admire. Together, they are a classic example of our preference for stationing ambulances at the bottom of cliffs rather than building fences at the top of them.

Are the Department of Education and Science, the Home Office, the Department of Health and Social Security and the Lord Chancellor's Department satisfied with these aspects of London's development and the G.L.D.P.? If London needs further special expenditure on educational, social, legal and policing services, will these Departments ensure that the funds required will be found? Should we be content if they do?

VII: PARTICIPATION

The defects of the evidence laid before the Inquiry make great difficulties for anyone concerned—as the GLC and the Panel clearly are—to enable the public to participate in planning. None of us can be expert in more than a small part of the immense field covered by the G.L.D.P.; but each of us understands a good deal, and cares a good deal, about the distribution of the Plan's benefits among people of various kinds and (which is much the same question) the distribution of the powers needed to put the Plan into action. Who gets the goodies? And who decides who gets the goodies? The public understands questions of this sort and wants to participate in debating them. (That is why there has been lively public debate about industrial relations, comprehensive schools, rent controls, motorway routes and other problems which pose these essentially political questions.)

The G.L.D.P. and the evidence about it given to the Inquiry have necessarily dealt at length with the technology of the Plan—its statistics, demography, econometrics and so on. But, through a kind of prudery, the *politics* of the Plan have scarcely been mentioned. Thus it has been difficult to discuss the distribution of different kinds of people across the map of London, and the access different groups will have to jobs, incomes, housing and other opportunities, and the distribution of power and responsibility for putting the plan into practice. That may be due to constraints imposed by statutory planning procedures, but the utter failure of the public to participate effectively in what should have been one of the great debates of the decade is the outcome. The questions which would have enabled people to participate have not been posed. People have not been treated as mature citizens. Not surprisingly, they have been bored and mystified by the whole procedure.

Chapter 4

People and Planning

PETER LEVIN and DAVID DONNISON

For a committee of twenty-six people to complete and publish a report on a difficult subject in sixteen months is a remarkable achievement. That their report should also be unanimous, humane, full of sensible proposals, well written and tellingly illustrated—all this is more remarkable still. We should be grateful to the Skeffington Committee for Britain's first official inquiry into 'the participation of the public' in town planning, and grateful to the Ministers who launched an investigation of problems which arise in equally pressing form (but have yet to be systematically studied) in many other branches of government.

Yet this report is only a beginning. Before long we shall have to press our inquiries and exert our capacities for political and administrative innovation a great deal further. To explain why the Skeffington Report is both important and inadequate calls for a brief account of recent developments in this country's approach to planning. Against this background the strengths and weaknesses of the Committee's proposals will be clearer. We can then look at some of the next problems on this agenda.

The Town and Country Planning Act of 1947 set up a centrally supervised and geographically comprehensive system of planning which lasted for more than twenty years. The local planning authorities—county councils and county borough councils—were given responsibility for controlling all development. They had to prepare development plans and submit them to the Minister (of Town and Country Planning, later Housing and Local Government) for approval. These plans were to be reviewed every five years and proposals for amendments submitted again to the Minister. Development plans had to show 'the manner in which the local planning authority propose that land in their area should be used'. Consequently they went into considerable detail, a tendency which grew as time passed. All these details were fed into a centralized system, with provision for public inquiry into objections (of which there might be hundreds or even thousands to a single plan). Thus it took the planning authorities years to prepare their plans, and the Ministry years to

approve them. By the time they were approved the plans were generally out-of-date in many ways.

In 1964 a Planning Advisory Group, composed mainly of central
and local government officials, was asked to reappraise this system.
Their report [1] pinpointed many of its defects: fundamental ones,
such as the amount of detail to be handled by an over-burdened
central administration, and the inadequacy of development plans
as instruments of regional planning; and consequential ones, such
as the lack of public confidence in the system. The Group proposed
that strategic policy decisions should be distinguished from detailed
tactical decisions and that each should be handled in different ways.
Development plans submitted to Ministers for approval should deal
only with the broad physical structure of the area and the principal
policies and priorities for its future development. The allocation of
sites for specific purposes and the details of implementation would
become the responsibility of the local planning authorities. The new
system should provide a real stimulus to public interest in planning
and give the authorities new opportunities for winning public support
for their proposals.

These proposals came at a point when many people had grasped
that the country's rates of demographic and economic growth were
likely to be much faster than anyone foresaw when the 1947 Act was
passed. *The South East Study*,[2] and other regional studies that
followed, showed the frightening volume of development to be
accommodated within a small island. Planners could no longer
assume the role of disinterested policemen, controlling this traffic;
they were taking increasing responsibilities for promoting and directing the flow of development. Meanwhile the geographical and
functional boundaries defining the job originally given to town planners were disintegrating. They had to play their part in economic
planning on a regional and national scale, and deal with transport
and communications, with the location of industry and the growth
and distribution of incomes, and with the impact made by planning
decisions on education, health, wild life, the pollution of the environment, and many other matters.

This increasingly comprehensive, purposeful and demanding
approach to planning was taking shape within a changing political
climate. The complacent assumption, widespread during the 1950s,
that full employment and the 'welfare state' had eliminated the main
social injustices was discredited. Attention was turning to the plight
of economically depressed regions, the poverty of larger families,
the growing numbers of homeless Londoners, racial discrimination
and educational deprivation.

A new generation, asking sharper questions about inequalities within the 'welfare state', was taking a more sceptical view than its predecessors of government and the public service professions. Earlier reformers, such as the Webbs, Tawney and Beveridge, had called for the expansion of the state's responsibilities and the professionalization of activities previously left in the hands of commercial or voluntary agencies. The creation of the town planning profession was itself an expression of this faith in the state and the professions serving it. But the new reformers were demanding clearer statements and stronger defences of the citizen's rights against government; they were suspicious of civil servants and official secrets; they criticized doctors and the health service, lawyers and the courts, social workers and social casework.

The Consumers' Association has grown more rapidly than any other voluntary organization during the past decade. It was a portent for the whole consumer movement. Other associations devoted themselves to the advancement of state education, the welfare of hospital patients, the building of co-operative housing, the improvement of public transport, and the preservation and enhancement of the rural and urban scene. 'Participation' became a word to conjure with in Britain, as it also was in France and the U.S.A.

Such were the developments which formed the climate in which the report of the Planning Advisory Group was received: rising concern about the scale of the nation's requirements for building and land; a daunting expansion of the scope and complexity of the planners' task; sharpening demands for social justice; demystification of government, and exposure of the professions to more insistent criticism; growing and better organized pressures for the improvement of public services and for public participation in their development. It was—and is—an invigorating climate, but an unsettled one: for planners it could be a stormy period.

The Planning Advisory Group's recommendations, with a commitment to public participation in planning, were embodied in the Town and Country Planning Act of 1968. The White Paper preceding the Act called for public discussion of important decisions 'while they are still at the formative stage and can be influenced by the people whose lives they affect'. When laying down the procedure for the preparation of structure plans before they are submitted to the Minister, the Act required the planning authority:

(a) to give 'adequate publicity to the report of the survey' that must be carried out;

89

(b) to inform anyone who might want to make representations on the subject that they have the opportunity to do so; and

(c) actually to provide that opportunity.

Even before the Act was passed, the Skeffington Committee was set up by the Ministry of Housing and Local Government 'to consider and report on the best methods, including publicity, of securing the participation of the public at the formative stage in the making of development plans for their area'. These are some of the main recommendations of their report, *People and Planning* [3]:

'People should be kept informed throughout the preparation of a structure or local plan for their area.'

'Representation should be considered continuously as they are made while plans are being prepared; but, in addition, there should be set pauses to give a positive opportunity for public reaction and participation. . . . Where alternative courses are available, the authority should put them to the public and say which it prefers and why.'

'Local planning authorities should consider convening meetings in their area for the purpose of setting up community forums. These forums would provide local organizations with the opportunity to discuss collectively planning and other issues of importance to the area. Community forums might also have administrative functions, such as receiving and distributing information on planning matters and promoting the formation of neighbourhood groups.'

'Community development officers should be appointed to secure the involvement of those people who do not join organizations. Their job would be to work with people, to stimulate discussion, to inform people and give people's views to the authority.'

'The public should be told what their representations have achieved or why they have not been accepted.'

'People should be encouraged to participate in the preparation of plans by helping with surveys and other activities as well as by making comments.'

These recommendations, elaborated in the report and illustrated in its appendices, should leave a lasting and constructive imprint on our planning procedures. The committee recognize that decisions are not made at the end of a process of survey, analysis and design, but evolve gradually with the accretion of commitment to particular courses of action. Hence consultation and rights of objection at the end of the process are not enough: by that stage the public must often accept something very like the planners' proposals if there is to be any action at all. Participation must start at the beginning of the process and continue throughout it. The Committee's assumption that 'surveys' will deal with people's needs, aspirations and opinions, as well as the geographical distribution of activities and land uses, is refreshing. Their assumption that survey results must be published is even more encouraging. They properly reject the view that particular professions, interests or voluntary associations should have a prescriptive right to be co-opted to planning committees. Their proposals for what amounts to a new political institution (a standing community forum) and a new official (the community development officer) are interesting, resembling in some ways the institutions and officials now being set up to deal with race relations.

But although these recommendations are good, so far as they go, we shall have to think harder and go further before long. The Committee do not seriously consider the possibility that participation and publicity may *frustrate* action: yet they must have known that St Giles Circus and the Euston Road were massively redeveloped in the utmost secrecy, while the squalor of Piccadilly Circus remains untouched—largely owing to the advance publicity given to proposals for its redevelopment.

They see participation as a pilgrim's progress, leading from ignorance and apathy to understanding, consensus and constructive action. The case for these assumptions is preached but never argued: participation and agreement are characteristic of the liberal-demo-cratic-unselfish society which is by definition the good society. But it could be argued that the public should choose representatives, committed to known general policies, who appoint competent staff to get on with the job: these professionals should then be accountable to their elected watchdogs alone. It could also be argued that conflict amongst the many interests in a complex urban society is inevitable, and can be resolved only by staging explicit public contests leading not to agreement but to compromise based on bargains.

It would be naive not to recognize that professionals have interests of their own at stake. They must avoid being 'caught out' in argument with laymen. They do not simply seek constructive action: they want visible achievements recognizably due to their own effort and skill. The highway engineer finds it more satisfying to build highways than to show that grade-separated intersections and an urban motorway are unnecessary. Every profession has its dogmas and shibboleths: shops must be grouped in precincts; building must not be 'monumental'; pedestrians and vehicles must be segregated; the London skyline must be preserved. These are not technical

91

criteria, leading inevitably to agreed solutions; they are slogans which enable every wealthy objector to find—somewhere or other—a duly qualified consultant willing to contest the proposals advanced by other members of his own profession. Understanding does not inevitably lead to goodwill and agreement: the better we understand some people, the less we like what we understand.

The ignorant, the apathetic and the helpless may as easily be neglected in the political market-places of participation as they are in the economic market-place of commerce. The Committee recognize this problem in saying that the community development officer 'would be primarily concerned with those who might not otherwise hear of proposals and take a part in influencing them'. But when we look for some serious discussion of the work of this officer, employed on the payroll of the politically powerful to represent and mobilize the politically powerless, we are disappointed to find the Committee saying, 'It would be quite wrong for us to try to say how he should work'.

In short, the Committee assume too readily that the conventions of a Quaker meeting can be adopted in the commercial, political, professional and racial rough-house in which planning decisions are actually made. It would be easy to conclude that their assumptions are more creditable than credible, but that would be unfair. They had to sell the idea of participation to town and county hall, to the professions, and to the public too. The first official report on this subject had to be an exercise in propaganda.

What should the next report deal with? It should more frankly clarify the aims of 'participation'. To give planners fuller information about human needs and aspirations? To mobilize pressures for prompt and effective action? To represent more effectively the minorities whose interests are neglected by conventional democratic procedures? To produce wiser and more responsible citizens? These are different and potentially conflicting objectives, to be pursued with different strategies.

We should examine the planning process more carefully and the ways in which planning decisions evolve. Such research would show, for example, that those whose needs are most likely to be neglected are not simply unrepresented (a problem which might be solved by political pressures and conventional procedures for legal aid)— they are often unknown. The future residents of a new town are un-identifiable; the future users of a school may be unborn. Planning inquiries conducted according to the adversary procedures inherited from the English courts may be quite inappropriate for dealing with decisions about such developments: inquisitorial procedures, based on a strengthened inspectorate armed with its own investigators, may sometimes be required.

Most of us could probably predict with some assurance the kind of people whose voices will be heard in the Skeffington Committee's community forum. To learn the needs of those who will not be heard, we shall have to make surveys of larger and more representative groups. Those interviewed could be formed into a panel, with a changing membership selected by purely random procedures of the kind adopted for BBC audience research. Besides using such panels for surveys of needs and activities, we might invite them to elect a committee, with the responsibilities proposed for the Skeffington Committee's community forum, which would choose some of the questions to be asked in surveys of panel members. (The planners may want to know how many people will use a car; the panel may be more anxious to know how many would use a nursery school.) The results of surveys, and the action later taken on the questions asked, would be publicly reported. The panel, and the local authority departments using the information derived from surveys of its members, would both need an independent and professionally competent third party (a university or a research firm) prepared to assure the reliability of the research methods employed and the confidentiality of the information given by individual respondents. To start with, a charitable trust might put up some of the money required to launch an experiment of this kind.

The Skeffington Committee say the findings of studies of the costs and benefits of alternative courses of action should more often be published. Again we must go further. Upon what kinds of people will the costs fall? To whom will the benefits accrue? Totals which do not reveal the *distributions* of costs and benefits often conceal the essential features of the decisions to be made.

These are some of the problems to which we must turn once public participation in planning seriously begins.

References

1. Planning Advisory Group, *The Future of Development Plans*, HMSO, 1965.
2. Ministry of Housing and Local Government, *The South East Study*, HMSO, 1964.
3. Report of the Committee on Public Participation in Planning, *People and Planning*, HMSO, 1969.

Chapter 5

Some Social Trends

PETER WILLMOTT

The purpose of this paper is to discuss some of the ways in which the social structure of Britain and the patterns of social life are likely to develop during the next two or three decades.[1] What has been happening in the past is obviously one guide to what is likely to happen in the future and the paper, taking this as its starting-point, begins by discussing past and present trends in the occupational structure and in social class. It then examines in particular the suggestion that the social class structure is fundamentally changing—that 'we are all middle class now' and likely to become even more so in the future. This is followed by a discussion of some trends in social relationships and behaviour, first in family life and secondly in social life outside the family. Finally, some of the major questions are posed and some suggestions offered on research priorities.

If one looks to the past for guidance and asks how British society has changed since, say, 1900, one comes face to face with a paradox. Put simply, it is that the social structure seems both to have changed radically and not to have changed very much.[2] This is particularly true of the occupational structure and social class.

OCCUPATIONS AND MOBILITY

The stereotype of what has happened to the British occupational structure since about 1900 is something like this: it has altered dramatically, particularly since 1945, the main changes being major shifts from unskilled to skilled occupations and from manual to clerical, with a large increase also in the professions and management.

In fact, as Routh shows in his *Occupation and Pay in Great Britain 1906–1960*,[3] the trends are much less dramatic than they are commonly thought. The proportion of clerical workers among working men, for instance, was 5 per cent in 1911 and 6 per cent in 1951. The proportion of professional men was 3 per cent in 1911, 6 per cent in 1951. The comparable figures for unskilled male manual

94

workers were 12 per cent in 1911, 14 per cent in 1951. In 1961 workers in 'manual' occupations, both men and women, still accounted for two-thirds of all the employed people in the United Kingdom.

Of course, there have been important changes in the economy. One is the entry of women into the labour force and the extent of the shift among them, much more marked than among men, from manual to clerical work. There have also been major changes, among men as well as women, between industries—notably the movement from agriculture, mining and textiles to new light industries, and the switch from manufacturing to services.

There is also some evidence that, despite the relatively slow rate of change until recently, the process may have speeded up quite sharply between 1951 and 1961.[4] In particular, the proportion of scientists, engineers and technologists in the United Kingdom increased by 56 per cent over that decade, and that of industrial technicians by 67 per cent. Between them, however, they still amounted to less than 3 per cent of the total labour force in 1961.

To the occupational changes already mentioned, others could be added. Manual work has, on the whole, become lighter, hours shorter, working conditions better and the structure of authority at work less oppressive. But in many respects the fundamental occupational structure seems relatively unchanged, especially for men. We may, as is sometimes suggested, be on the brink of major changes in technology that will radically transform that structure. All one can say is that the experience of the past fifty years or so should encourage caution.[5]

Another common assumption is that there is now much more movement across occupational strata from one generation to the next—that more sons of carpenters and dockers than in the past become managers and surgeons. The latest figures on this are not very up to date; they come from the study in 1949 by Glass and his colleagues at the London School of Economics, whose findings were published in 1954.[6] This study showed virtually no change, as compared with the end of the last century, in the extent of inter-generational mobility in Britain. As Glass put it, the general picture was of 'rather high stability over time'.[7] A review by Lipset and Bendix, drawing on historical data from a number of other industrial countries, also found little change over a period of about forty years.[8] A more recent study of American society, by Blau and Duncan, came to the same general conclusion.[9] With occupational mobility, as with the broad occupational structure, the main impression is therefore that society has changed less than is commonly supposed.

95

EDUCATION AND WEALTH

At first sight, education presents a different picture. For one thing, there is clearly more of it. The proportion of 14-year-olds at school in England and Wales was 9 per cent in 1902 and 30 per cent in 1938. By 1954, 32 per cent of 15-year-olds were at school and ten years later 59 per cent. The proportion aged 15 to 19 in grant-aided schools went up from 10 per cent in 1956 to 19 per cent in 1967.[10] The numbers in full-time education in England and Wales have more than trebled in the past twenty years and nearly doubled in the last ten alone.

All this does not of course necessarily mean that working-class children are now getting a larger *share* of university places. What has apparently happened is that working and middle classes alike are benefiting from university expansion; their relative shares are, or at any rate were at the beginning of the 1960s, similar to what they used to be in earlier periods. The Robbins Report showed that, of 18-year-olds from non-manual homes, 8·9 per cent entered university in 1928 to 1947 and 16·8 per cent in 1960; from manual homes, 1·4 per cent of the 18-year-olds entered in 1928 to 1947 and 2·6 per cent in 1960.[11] While later figures would show higher proportions for both, there is no reason to think that the relative shares have changed.

In other words, despite the changes, the divisions of social class are still formidable. It is, as far as one can judge, much the same with wealth and income. Meade has shown that there has been little change in the distribution of wealth in Britain: the proportion of total personal wealth owned by the richest 5 per cent was 79 per cent in 1936–8 and 75 per cent in 1960.[12] On incomes, the changes are more difficult to trace. But Routh shows that there was little change between 1911–12 and 1958–59 in the share of incomes, both before and after tax, by the different occupational strata.[13] Nicholson's study suggests little radical change in the distribution of income over recent years.[14] Furthermore, Titmuss has pointed out that 'fringe' benefits—firm's cars, housing, school fees, pensions, etc.—ought to be taken into account, and that if they were the better off would undoubtedly be shown to benefit most from them.[15]

These facts point to two general impressions about the last half century. The first is that, despite some changes, the social structure has in some of the essentials remained extraordinarily constant. The second is that this is particularly true in terms of social class.

THE OTHER SIDE

That is only part of the story. If one looks at it the other way round and asks how people's day-to-day lives have changed, the impression is utterly different. As is well known, living standards have risen. Mass production has put into the hands of the many what were formerly the privileges of the few. Social policy has plainly helped as well; the 'price' of primary and secondary education and that of health services have been fixed at zero, and social security has aided the poorest.

As a result of all this there has undoubtedly been some 'convergence' in tastes, consumption and behaviour within British society. There has also been an improvement in the social status of manual workers and their families.[16] And there is a ring of truth in Marshall's suggestion that social inequality has been reduced over the past three centuries by the spread of 'citizenship' among the social classes, characteristically through 'civil rights' in the eighteenth century, 'political rights' in the nineteenth and 'social rights' in the twentieth.[17]

This then is the paradox—the mixture of change and 'unchange' in the British social structure, particularly in terms of social class. How is one to reconcile these apparently contradictory trends and not only make sense of what has happened but, more relevant, make sound judgements about what may happen over the next two or three decades?

Clearly both sets of trends are likely to continue. First, despite the current economic setbacks, we are likely to get richer and, compound growth being what it is, at an accelerating rate. As Abrams has put it, in stating the first of his 'assumptions' about consumption in the year 2000:

> ... it is assumed that the average standard of living in Britain will be substantially higher in the year 2000 than it is in 1967; reasonably, it may be double; and, very optimistically it may have trebled. Within these limits the precise measure of growth, however, is not important; whatever the rate of increase, the broad mass of the population at the end of the century will have incomes that today are enjoyed by only a minority of richer households.[18]

That is an assumption that this paper makes also. Yet the relative shares of wealth and income by different sections of the population are unlikely to change fundamentally. In other words, though all will be richer, 'inequality' will not be reduced; indeed it may well increase. Meade demonstrates convincingly that there is a fundamental conflict between economic efficiency and what he calls 'distributional justice' [19]: the greater the emphasis on economic growth, therefore —and it is likely to dominate national policy in the decades ahead as much as in the recent past—the greater the pressures towards

97

economic inequality. For this reason, another of Abrams's 'assumptions' seems more questionable than the one already quoted. This second 'assumption' is that in the year 2000 'the distribution of net personal total incomes will be more equal than it is today'.[20]

Enough has been said to show that it would be a mistake to assume this. The example brings into sharp focus the two contradictory elements—the trend towards some sort of social equality and cultural homogeneity, and the tendency for many of the essentials of the British social structure to stay as they are. With this theme in mind, the paper now looks in more detail at some emerging social patterns.

ECONOMIC GROWTH AND STANDARDS OF LIVING

First, a closer look at what has happened to standards of living. As is well known, Britain's Gross National Product has been increasing, with some short-term ups and downs, since the 1880s. Real incomes have risen at the same time. Consumer spending has been increasing at least since 1900/5 and particularly since 1945; it rose by over a fifth between 1950 and 1960.[21]

The biggest proportionate increases in consumer spending since 1900 have been in 'transport' and 'entertainment'. Spending on most other things has increased too. More and more working-class families have bought, as well as cars, household equipment like washing machines, refrigerators and television sets. This is especially noticeable with housing. More working-class people live in modern homes; a quarter of our housing stock has been built since 1945. More own their homes: Donnison, using data from surveys in 1958 and 1962, has shown how much home-ownership increased over those four years alone. The proportion of skilled manual workers owning or buying their own houses went up from 33 per cent to 39 per cent, and of unskilled and semi-skilled from 20 per cent to 26 per cent.[22]

It seems reasonable to assume that this process will continue—that the Gross National Product will rise and, with it, household incomes and living standards. As a broad guide one can accept Abrams's suggestion, referred to earlier, that the average standard of living is likely to rise by the year 2000 to somewhere between double and treble what it is now.

Past experience seems a fairly good pointer to the main ways in which the extra consumers' income will be spent. The 130-year-old dictum described by Bell as 'Tocqueville's Law'—'What the few have today, the many will demand tomorrow' [23]—seems to have been largely borne out by events. Though of course an over-simplification, it has proved not at all a bad general indication of likely future trends in consumption and patterns of life.

Thus many features of what is now middle-class life are likely to spread. More cars, more household equipment, more suburban-style homes and communities would not surprise anyone. Modern societies (perhaps to some extent all societies) seem to be characterised by a continuing process of 'diffusion', by which some values and patterns of behaviour percolate 'downwards' through the social strata. Some examples of change in food consumption in the nineteenth century have been recently cited:

> The growth of town-living encouraged competition and social imitation among all classes, leading ultimately to far more sophisticated tastes and eating habits. The outstanding examples of this are white bread and tea, both of which were, in the eighteenth century, the luxuries of the well-to-do.[24]

Of course some diffusion is 'upwards'—one example is the dining-kitchen, originally a peasant and then an urban working-class pattern which is now fashionable, with the decline in domestic help, among the colour-supplement middle class. Some diffusion, and probably an increasing proportion, is not so much across social strata as across age-groups—fashions in men's clothes, for instance, often move not from 'top' class to 'bottom' but from young to old. Perhaps in general the greater degree of homogeneity over a certain span of the standard of living means that 'fashion' will in certain spheres increasingly take the place of the steady 'downward' drift from rich to poor. Yet over large areas of life, the latter kind of diffusion clearly still sets the style and will continue to do so.

It seems that diffusion is a cumulative process; that acquiring, for example, a car or a house of one's own can lead to changes in behaviour. Thus a working-class man living with his family in a 'semi' in the suburbs is more likely to live like his middle-class neighbour than like a man who is his neighbour only at work and still lives in an Islington slum. A Stevenage capstan operator with a Cortina is likely to use his car for shopping, for holidays, for family visits and Sunday 'drives into the country', and from the side of the road at any rate is indistinguishable from his white-collar counterpart in Hertford or Hitchin. As more manual workers own homes and cars, people's patterns of life will merge further.

The process is surely encouraged by TV and the other mass media which, whatever one's final judgement about their influence for good or evil, help to make for cultural homogeneity, by bringing the same models of behaviour into the homes of people in all strata. We increasingly share in a broad national, in some respects international, culture—the 'global village'. It is a matter for speculation how far regional, local and class sub-cultures can continue to survive in such a setting, and how far we can preserve 'pluralism', the 'diversity within unity' that seems so desirable. It is possible that the recent upsurge of Celtic nationalism represents some sort of reaction against the growth of cultural uniformity, and in that sense testifies to the extent to which cultural homogeneity has already taken hold. There are, of course, still important variations in behaviour, in values and in tastes, not only as between different occupational or economic strata and different kinds of people within them but also as between the different regions of Britain (some of them striking).[25] In some respects, too, contemporary British society encompasses more 'deviance' and more variety than in the past. At the same time the general trend is clearly towards a broad homogeneity, over the great majority of the population, in consumption patterns and in social behaviour.

SOCIAL CLASS AND LIFE-STYLES

How can these suggestions be reconciled with the warning earlier— that in many fundamental ways the social structure remains unchanged? The key seems to lie in a distinction, first made by Weber, between people's situation in the economic structure and their 'style of life', reflecting their consumption standards and social patterns outside work.[26]

The difference between the work situations of manual workers and others is marked, and this difference affects values and behaviour. A study in Luton by Lockwood and his colleagues found, for instance, that most manual workers recognized that their prospects of personal advancement in their work (i.e. of promotion) were negligible.[27] Manual workers know that almost their only hope of economic advance is in the company of their fellows. Since they are paid by the week or hour, their security is limited. The middle-class man can with more justification see his job as a career-ladder up which, if all goes well, he will climb as he gets older, and he usually gets more 'satisfaction' from his work. The working-class man may or may not like work; either way he sees it mainly as a means of earning a living. To the middle-class man work, or advancement in work, is more often the 'central life interest', to borrow Dubin's phrase.[28]

There are a number of other related differences. Working-class people, for obvious reasons deriving from their work situation, are disposed to collective rather than individual action to achieve economic advance.[29] Similarly, the attitude of most working-class men to politics seems relatively 'traditional', tied to class attitudes.[30]

There is some evidence, too, that the working-class view of leisure is rather different from the middle-class. Here it seems that the gap between the classes may in some respect be widening. Reisman has suggested that some members of the middle class, particularly professional people, increasingly see their leisure as 'instrumental'; for example, they use their social life to promote contacts with colleagues and professional clients, or they read the newspapers with an eye to their work interests. Manual workers, by contrast, are said increasingly to separate work and leisure.[31] Nevertheless, as is shown later, what people actually *do* in their leisure seems to vary less, and many middle-class patterns of leisure behaviour are likely to spread.

In some other aspects of social life there are still sharp class differences. In the old districts the familiar working-class attachments to kinship and neighbourhood die hard,[32] and even in the new areas substantial elements of the old life survive or are re-established.[33] As the Luton study shows, working-class people also remain unlike middle-class for instance in belonging less often to formal organizations. In particular they certainly do not 'become middle-class' in the sense of mixing with white-collar workers.[34] Our own study in Woodford even suggested that in a suburb where there was a growing homogeneity of life-styles, the middle-class residents were increasingly inclined to lay emphasis on the small social differences that distinguished them from their working-class neighbours.[35]

MERGING OF SOCIAL CLASSES

To sum up so far, it is clear that in some respects the classes are 'merging' but also that there are limits to the process. In general, life outside work has changed more than life inside it. Diffusion, it seems, is more likely to occur with consumption patterns than with basic values linked to political attitudes or class loyalties.

Something more can be said about the influences upon such values. The Luton study suggests that though 'traditional' class and political loyalties may be somewhat influenced by 'affluence'—that is, that higher-paid workers are somewhat more inclined to vote Conservative—there is a much closer correlation with family affiliations. The manual workers whose fathers or fathers-in-law have non-manual backgrounds, whose wives work in white-collar jobs or who themselves have had such jobs in the past—these are markedly more likely to support the Conservatives than others without such links.[36] There is ample evidence that the type of community has an influence too, that in a homogeneous working-class community the 'traditional'

101

loyalties and values hold more sway than they do, for example, in a mixed-class suburb.[37]

In discussing what is likely to happen, these various influences have to be reckoned with. The first suggestion is the familiar one: that, in patterns of consumption and in associated behaviour, middle-class styles are likely to spread. The second is that changes in behaviour—and to some extent in values—will also be influenced by the extent of geographical mobility and even more by changes in the occupational structure (which are likely gradually to reduce the proportion of manual occupations and increase the proportion of families having some links with white-collar milieux).

The limits to the process of class 'merging' have been noted and are obviously substantial. It would clearly be wrong to talk as if the working class was near to extinction. Even more important, increasing affluence and 'bourgeoisification' will not in themselves eradicate poverty. First, there is the point made earlier that national emphasis on economic growth will if anything lead to a less equitable distribution of income and wealth. Secondly, even if the distribution of national income does not become less equitable, there will, as long as there are any variations in incomes, continue to be a distribution 'curve' and therefore a poorest 10 per cent or 25 per cent; in this sense, 'poverty' is obviously common to all industrial societies. Thirdly, even in the richest societies, some of the poorer strata remain so locked in a vicious circle of economic and social deprivation that they combine together in a 'culture' or, more correctly, 'sub-culture of poverty'; they thus remain in important senses excluded from the national society. It seems that in certain conditions economic expansion, far from reducing this sense of exclusion, may actually sharpen it and thus deepen social divisions.

We do not know whether the sense of 'relative deprivation' will grow. It certainly does not seem strong in British society at present. Reporting his 1962 survey, Runciman said: 'On the evidence of this question, relative deprivation is low in both magnitude and scope even among those who are close to the bottom of the hierarchy of economic class.' [38] But this may change with increasing cultural homogeneity and with increasing emphasis upon economic prosperity, national and personal, as the key index of achievement.

There are minorities of colour as well as of income. Again nobody can predict with any confidence whether the coloured minorities will, as they improve their lot, actually become more embittered about what they lack because of their skin colour—as has happened in the United States. Nor whether the same improvements may not sharpen the sense of 'relative deprivation' on the part of poor whites. What does seem likely is that the two linked problems of poverty and colour will continue and questions of income distribution and differential opportunity grow in importance at the same time as living standards rise generally.

FAMILY AND HOME

The paper now looks more closely at some particularly important changes in patterns of behaviour. First, the family. The kind of diffusion mentioned earlier affects the family as it does other social institutions. Despite the continuing role of kinship, there is increasing stress upon the immediate family and particularly the husband-wife relationship. The shift is from the 'consanguine' family, emphasizing ties of kinship, to the 'conjugal', emphasizing the husband-wife bond. It is clear that this pattern is becoming increasingly dominant, spreading 'downwards' from the middle class inside each country and from the richer to the poorer countries, as part of the growing 'Westernization' of the world.[39]

One of the most striking trends in Britain, as in much of the rest of the world, is the growing popularity of family life. In the 1920s about 80 per cent of women could expect eventually to marry [40]; now the proportion is 95 per cent.[41] Marriages also now start at an earlier age: among women aged 20 to 24, in 1921 27 per cent were married; in 1961 58 per cent.[42] Because of the longer expectation of life, marriages end later as well.

The change in the 'life-cycle' of marriage is shown in Table 1 (this is based upon assessments of the available demographic data, which are not all that one would like).[43]

Table 1   *Family Life-Cycle 'Profile' for Women in England and Wales, 1911, 1951 and 1967*

	1911	1951	1967
Women's mean age at first marriage	26	25	23
Women's mean age when last child born	34	28	27
Women's mean age at husband's death	54	63	65
Women's mean age at death as a widow	73	78	80

These figures show a transformation in marriage. Marriages start earlier, as noted above, and last longer. The 'average' marriage, if wives outlived their husbands, lasted 28 years in 1911 and 42 years in 1967. If one assumes that children cease to be fully dependent at 15, then the period when the couple are largely alone has changed even more—from five years in 1911 to 23 years in 1967. The figures indicate that, in contrast with the earlier period, about as much of a

103

couple's family life is now spent without dependent children as with.[44]

Some years ago Titmuss, using rather different calculations, pointed out the implications of this change for the status of women,[45] and the effect is shown in the change in the employment of married women, which has been touched on earlier. The proportions of wives working has gone up in Britain from 9 per cent in 1921 [46] to 27 per cent in 1951 and again to 40 per cent in 1966.[47] The biggest increase has been among wives aged 35 to 44.

This means, for an increasing proportion, a different sort of marriage and a different sort of family life. Instead of the husband going away for long hours at work, leaving the wife at home with the children, more of marriage involves their both going out of the home (the wife for at least some of the time), working together in the home and sharing their leisure time together.[48] The demographic change is an expression of the growth of partnership in marriage and has also helped to encourage it.

The partnership takes three main forms. First, it is a partnership in power, with major decisions being discussed and made jointly. Secondly, it is a partnership in the division of labour within the home, as the old distinctions between men's and women's jobs (though still made) become increasingly blurred. More wives go out to work and help paint the kitchen; more husbands take the children out in the pram and help wash the nappies. Thirdly, it is a partnership in social life, with couples spending more of their free time together and with their children. One could sum up by saying that, despite the inequalities that remain between the sexes, women now have higher status, and that there is greater equality in society and in the family. Children, too, have a higher status.[49]

The changes in social roles inside marriage reflect a more general tendency. As a recent article on American society points out, in dress and hair styles the sexes are more alike than they have usually been in the past; men now spend more than women on perfumed preparations; boys and girls are increasingly given 'ambisexual' names.[50] In all sorts of ways, in Britain and in the United States, the sexes are becoming more alike and sex roles less 'polarized'.

Associated with the changes in family relationships is a trend towards what has been called the 'home-centred' society.[51] For most families homes are more spacious and better equipped. More time is spent in the home and a number of trends support and encourage this. Television, for instance, means that the family can be entertained—or bored—together in the home, instead of separately in the cinema.

In studies of three contrasted communities in East London, three stages of this process were noted. In Bethnal Green, the established working-class community in the East End, there was a change compared with earlier decades—a shift towards the home and towards marriage partnership. In the new housing estate of 'Greenleigh', to which ex-Bethnal Greeners had moved, the process had gone a stage further.[52] The middle-class couples of suburban Woodford were further still along the same path.[53] This comparison suggests two generalizations. First, this is another example of class transmission, with the working-class following the middle. (There is, however, no neat correlation between class and marriage partnership; it seems that among the most 'successful' professional and managerial people many spend less time at home, help less around the house and are in some respects as far from 'partnership' as are unskilled workers.) Secondly, the example illustrates how the change can be accelerated: in working-class families the move to the new community and the break with the old helps to hasten the process of diffusion.

One general question has to be posed about this process: will the changes to family and home in fact continue along the present lines, or will the next few decades see instead a reaction against the family, as Leach has suggested? [54] Certainly there are likely to be some modifications. The 'Dual-Career Family', described by the Rapoports,[55] is likely to become more common, and at the same time the demand will grow for domestic arrangements that help it, including perhaps family 'service houses' like those appearing in Denmark and Sweden. Also, as living standards rise, children are likely to withdraw from the family circle at an earlier age and in particular more young people are going to demand the residential independence that their better-off fellows already enjoy. Even inside the home, there is likely to be greater emphasis on personal privacy and individuation, which involves more space, better internal soundproofing, personal record players, television sets and telephones.

It is possible that the family may change more dramatically, that, as Leach suggests, some variant of the Israeli kibbutz or the Chinese commune may take the place of the present form of family.[56]

However, the present trends seem so powerful, so world-wide, that it is hard to believe that Leach is right. What seems much more likely is that, with some modification, the shift to home-centredness and family-centredness will continue. The two sets of changes reinforce each other; the changes in family relationships and the shift to home-centredness increase the demand for a suitable home, and the 'home-and-garden' life further encourages home and family-centredness. More and more people will choose to take part of their higher real

105

incomes in the form of a home of their own. More and more families will have their own swimming pools and tennis courts, garages and workshops. All in all, the next thirty years or so are likely to see an ever-growing demand from an increasing number of families for separate spacious homes with gardens and for the lives that go with them. The suburban way of life may be expected to spread to more sections of the population.

Yet there may be a counter-trend to urban spread. The long period that couples now have and will have without children and the increase in wives working may between them somewhat check the rush to the suburbs. For one thing, since the average married couple are spending as much of their lifetime without dependent children as with them, many may be willing as they get older to exchange their three- or four-bedroomed house with garden for a smaller dwelling. Secondly, wives who work may prefer to give up suburban life for the greater accessibility to work they can find in inner areas.

FAMILY SIZE AND POPULATION SIZE

A question mark hangs over another aspect of family structure—family size. This is important for the future of urban life. The pressures on space, described earlier, will intensify even more, particularly in the most crowded regions, if the population grows rapidly. Of the population increase from 1961 to 1981 forecast in *The South East Study*, more than two-thirds was due to the growth in the Region's existing population, less than one-third to migration from other parts of the country.[57] But population projections for the end of the century (vital as they evidently are) could well be out by many millions either way—representing an immense variation in the demand for new housing, new road systems, new amenities.

This is because population size is so difficult to predict. Mortality and even migration are relatively easy to forecast; the big unknown is the birth-rate. The post-war 'Baby Boom', at first thought to be temporary, seemed to have ended in about 1952. But the birth-rate started to rise again in 1956 and through to the early 1960s. Time and again over those years, as the latest figures for births came in, the Government Actuary had to raise his sights. Over the past two or three years, however, the birth-rate has fallen; the estimates have been revised again, this time downwards.

What nobody knows is what lies behind these variations in birth-rate, yet this is just what we need to know to improve our guesses about the future. The increase in the marriage rate and the lower marriage age, referred to earlier, are apparently part of the explana-

106

tion, but only part: the Registrar General has estimated that, of the increase in legitimate births between 1955 and 1962, the increase in the number of married women accounted for 12 per cent and earlier marriage for 21 per cent, leaving 67 per cent due to more births per family.[58] Thus the crucial two questions remain: why have couples had more children and what is likely to happen over the coming decades? To answer the first may go some way to answering the second.

One key to the answer lies in the change in the relationship between social class and family size. In the second half of the nineteenth century, the upper and middle classes led the way in controlling conception, and for about seventy or eighty years there was a clear-cut negative correlation between social class and family size. The lower the class, the larger the family. The correlation held throughout the century because family size fell more or less proportionately in all classes.

After 1940, as the birth-rate in general showed its first real rise, a new pattern began to emerge. In Britain and in the United States, the very sections of the population who had in earlier generations limited family size most effectively now started having more children. The 1951 Census confirmed the trend and the 1961 Census suggested that certain professional groups in particular were drawing still further ahead. Thus the larger-than-average families are now to be found among the professional classes and the unskilled, among some of the richest as well as some of the poorest sections of the population. There is a similar correlation with education: the most educated and the least have families larger than the average. Though the Pill may cause some check in the birth-rate (and may partly explain the recent fall) it does not follow that it will lead to a long-term decline in family size; many of the professionals having large families are apparently doing so not because they cannot control conception but because they want to have children.

Why this is so is a matter for speculation. One hypothesis is that at some level of material prosperity (absolute or relative) the 'value', or what might be called the marginal utility, of an extra child is greater (i.e. gives more satisfaction) than alternative ways of spending one's money.[59] Having relatively large numbers of children (which means, nowadays, having four instead of two) seems also to be associated with a sense of economic security and of confidence about one's future. Two points are worth noting. First, professional people, above all others in our society, have reasonable expectations that as they get older their income will rise fairly steeply; not so the manual worker, who apart from general advances can expect no more at 55 than at 25, or the clerk, who can expect only modest increments. Secondly, it has been plausibly suggested that since the war the national birth-rate has fluctuated with levels of economic growth and employment (with people postponing births until the hoped-for better times return) and that the recent falling-off in births may be a reflection of Britain's economic difficulties in the past year or two.[60]

The central issue is whether family size will prove another example of class diffusion. As the unskilled follow the skilled manual workers in becoming skilled, at any rate about contraception, will a second and contrary wave spread 'downwards' through society? Will greater prosperity lead the clerks, then the skilled workers, and eventually the unskilled to turn back towards larger families as the professional people have already done? One would guess not, unless the occupational structure changes so radically that the lathe operator has as much security and can expect, as he gets older, as 'progressive' a climb in income as the architect or university teacher. In other words, it seems that family size is one aspect of life-style which depends more on work-situation and career prospects than on living-standards. But we cannot be sure. On this issue so central to future urbanization, since we do not know the reasons for what is happening now, we cannot be at all confident in guessing what may happen in the future.

LEISURE TIME

From the general discussion of family and home, it might appear that people's interests are becoming narrowed down. More time is spent in the home: with television, telephones, deep freezers and the like, more activities can take place there—entertainment, education, even work. All this might seem to point to a future in which there is relatively little mobility. As is well known, however, there is also a contrary trend. As well as the concentration inside the home, there is also the tendency to go longer distances when outside it. This is likely to continue.

These changes are associated with the increase in leisure time. People have—and will have—more time to spend in the home, but also more to spend outside it. The 'standard working week' has fallen from the 60 hours that became general when the 'ten-hour' day was secured in the 1840s to 48 after the First World War, 44 after the Second, 42 in 1960 and 40 today. The fall in the actual hours worked has, because of overtime, been much less marked. Indeed, the average has remained fairly stable over the past 30 years.[61] There are some suggestions that professional people may work longer hours than in the past.[62]

Another *caveat* is about second jobs—'moonlighting'. It seems that some people, faced with the prospect of more leisure, prefer to fill this time with extra work (and earn extra money) instead. The rubber workers in the American town of Akron have enjoyed a six-hour day since the 1930s; Swados, studying them, found that the extra leisure was not always welcomed and that moonlighting was common.[63] Wilensky, in another American study, found that one in ten of middle-class employees currently had a second job and one in three had been a 'moonlighter' at some time in the past.[64]

Thus there are likely in the future to be some people who choose to fill their time with second jobs and others, mainly senior professionals and managers, who continue to find long hours essential to a successful career. These apart, the general long-term trend is unmistakable—for most people, the proportion of total time spent at work can be expected to continue to fall over the coming decades.

So far the discussion of free time has been solely in terms of hours worked per week. The balance of work and non-work time can be discussed in a number of other ways. One perspective is that of the life-cycle: if less time in total needs to be spent at work, then people could start work later in life and finish earlier—they might stay longer in full-time education or they might retire earlier. Both trends are already evident, and it is reasonable to predict that they will continue. In particular, more young people are likely to stay longer in further education. In addition, the expected changes in technology and in the occupational structure will mean that more and more adults will later in life need (and want) to re-enter the educational process in one way or another, often including some full-time study.

The division of work and non-work time can also be looked at on an annual basis. If less time is needed at work, there are broadly these choices:

(a) Shorter hours each day;
(b) Less days at work each week;
(c) Longer annual holidays.

What seems to have happened in the last twenty years or so is that the emphasis has been on the last two rather than the first. In 1945 the five-day week was the exception; now it is almost universal. Annual paid holidays increased in most industries from one to two weeks in the 1950s; now nearly half of all manual workers have a paid holiday of more than two weeks.[65]

It seems probable that leisure time will continue to extend in these forms. Thus, for example, the 30-hour week, when it comes, is more likely to take the form of a four-day week than a six-hour day.

109

Annual holidays are in general already longer for non-manual workers, especially professional and managerial,[66] than manual, and the expected long-term changes in the occupational structure will encourage the existing trend to longer paid holidays.

It is worth noting that these trends in the division of leisure time fit in with the home-centred life described earlier. If the husband in particular has a lengthy journey to work, it is better for him and for the family if he can concentrate his work-life into a limited number of days each week and keep whole days free for home and family. It is at the weekend, above all, that family life comes into its own. And large slices of holiday, away from work and with the family instead, are also well suited to a society that values family life so highly.

SECOND HOMES, HOLIDAYS AND TRAVEL

Much of the leisure outside the home is—and will continue to be—still in a family setting. With many activities the impression is that the strongest wish is to create another miniature 'home' elsewhere. The family car can be seen as a sort of home on wheels even without a caravan and, when the children are young, very much one for the whole family. Many recreational activities now increasing in popularity—for example, caravanning, cruising and sailing—are things that families usually do together. The impression is also that there is an increase in 'independent' family holidays—families renting chalets, country cottages, seaside flats, Mediterranean villas.

'Second homes' are an even more obvious means of combining family life with frequent 'holidays', and though firm evidence is sparse, these are surely on the increase. In a recent small survey in London in which 100 people were interviewed, we found a marked difference according to social class in the ownership of country cottages and other second homes. In a middle-class area of Kensington, a quarter of households had a second home, compared with none in a working-class area of Hackney. But among the latter, two-thirds expressed the desire for one as did over half the Kensington people without one. This and more substantial evidence [67] suggest that with rising living standards, a growing proportion of town-dwellers will acquire second homes, and a growing proportion of leisure time, mainly weekends and annual holidays, will be spent in them, either in Britain or abroad.

In addition, as more families get cars and higher real incomes, there will be an increase in travel and holidays generally. In 1967, according to the Family Expenditure Survey,[68] households whose 'head' was

110

middle-class in occupation, as compared with those whose 'head' was a manual worker, spent 76 per cent more on 'private motoring' and nearly three times as much on 'holidays, hotels, etc.'. These are clear pointers to future growths in demand. So as well as the growing importance of home and family in leisure, there will also be an increase in mobility, including family mobility. More time and money will go into travel for social and recreational purposes, into holidays in hotels and the like, into rented holiday homes of various kinds, and into second family homes.

LEISURE AND GEOGRAPHICAL DISPERSAL

The likely developments in leisure patterns are discussed in a paper by H. B. Rodgers.[69] The main point here is that much of the growth is expected to be in recreations that need large quantities of space. With the expected increase in population, space is in any case likely to become more precious, particularly in the heavily-populated areas like the South East. Thus the result will be that more people will have to travel much longer distances for their golf, dinghy sailing, riding or countryside walking. The value of open country and seclusion is likely to increase, along with the price that people have to pay, in travel time, to reach it. This will further encourage the trends noted earlier—more time at home (whether first or second home), and longer distance travel when outside it.

The development of mass education and the influence of television and other mass media have also helped to awaken appetites for new and more specialized interests, ones that depend on a larger population to draw from and on a large catchment area. Increasingly people, as individuals this time rather than as family members, travel longer distances to engage in specialized interests. All this represents a greater variety and more choice. As was noted earlier, changes like these represent a qualification to the general picture of growing social homogeneity; it seems that we are moving both towards a greater homogeneity in certain areas of life and towards an increasing diversity in others. In any case, because of improved communications, the trend is indisputably away from the 'place community' and towards what Webber has called the 'interest community'.[70]

Of course, it does not follow that the 'place community', i.e. the local community, is going to be rubbed out by the ease of communications. It continues to figure importantly in most people's lives. Its significance varies among other things by age, sex, social class, income and car ownership: on the whole women's social contacts, being more tied to the home, are less dispersed than men's; those of young children, of their parents and of old people are less dispersed than those of other people and those of unmarried adolescents and young adults most dispersed of all; those of car owners more than of people without cars; those of middle-class and richer people more than working-class and poorer. These variations showed up in the small pilot study in London already mentioned, when people were asked what was the longest journey they had made during the previous month. For example, among working-class people one in seven had made a journey of 100 miles or more; among middle-class people the proportion was over a third; in particular, among middle-class people earning £3,000 or more a year it was well over half. Such local ties as there are differ too: for instance, they may be mainly with relatives (as in working-class areas) or with friends (as in middle-class). Furthermore, the proportion of a person's total social contacts that are local as against those that are dispersed varies along similar sex, age and class lines.

This suggests a continuing role for local community, even among many for whom local relationships account for only a relatively small part of their social life as a whole. But it does also suggest that a whole series of pressures—higher living standards, more cars, more education—are likely once again to cause middle-class styles of life to spread, mobility to increase and dispersed 'interest communities' to flourish still more.

* * *

This paper has suggested that, although the social structure of Britain seems relatively unchanging, especially in terms of the shares and opportunities of different social classes, there is a long-term general trend for middle-class tastes and consumption patterns to spread, for patterns of life and culture to become in some important respects more homogeneous. In particular, as one example of this homogeneity, the growth of partnership marriage and home-centredness has been noted. It has also been suggested, as another example, that travel will increase and with it the importance of geographically dispersed 'interest communities', which means that the greater homogeneity in one respect (dispersal becoming more common) will mean greater heterogeneity in another (more variety of interests). The paper ends by discussing the relevance to patterns of urbanization of these two trends in turn and raising some major questions that remain.

HOMES AND SUBURBS

The shift towards home and family suggests that the spread of the city (if it can still be called that) will accelerate. The trends are already clearly evident—in what has happened around London and other large British cities and in the experience of the United States—and it seems as if nothing can stop the process of further dispersal as living standards rise, even more so if at the same time the population increases substantially. It seems that something like Los Angeles is bound to be the urban model for Britain's future.

But there are some doubts. People want—or think they want—large houses and gardens in suburbs, exurbs or new towns. When they get them they have still not arrived in Paradise. The evidence on this is somewhat contradictory. Gans seems to have found in his study of *The Levittowners*,[71] a high degree of satisfaction with suburbia, though some of his interpretations might be regarded as tendentious. Other studies, mainly in Britain, show general 'contentment', particularly with the new house, but also strong criticism, particularly by wives, of loneliness, of the absence of shops, entertainment and other amenities, and of public transport.[72]

On the journey to work in particular there is again some apparent conflict. Gans states that most of the Levittowners he studied did not mind a long journey to work, though he did find that nearly two-thirds had a journey of over 40 minutes and that 30 per cent of those taking 40 to 59 minutes 'disliked' it, as did 44 per cent of those taking an hour or more.[73] Our own study in Ipswich showed that, of the people whose journey to work took over 20 minutes, a third considered the journey 'inconvenient'. And in our recent pilot interviews in the London area, again a third of those living in suburban areas said they 'disliked' the journey to work. Certainly on the face of it one would assume that, although some people might actually enjoy a long journey to work, many commuters resent the loss of leisure time. They have to surrender a large proportion of the very 'family life' for which they have moved.

The issue is whether an acceptable environment could be provided for family life, something with the essential elements of the 'home-and-garden' but without a continuing geographical spread. The question is pointed up by the other demands for space in and around cities. The growth in car ownership means more space will be needed for parking and for roads. Higher standards mean larger school sites and playing fields. Changing tastes in recreation generate extra 'needs'. Golf courses and marinas may soon be 'essentials'.

These pressures mean that we must at least question whether suburbanization is inevitable, or whether it would be possible to strike a balance that would more successfully meet people's needs. Two trends that have been noted earlier might encourage the alternative to Los Angeles: the changing family structure which might create a growing demand for smaller, garden-less dwellings, and the increase

113

in wives working which might make more attractive the greater accessibility of inner urban areas.

There is also the predicted growth in second homes: it is possible that, particularly with a longer weekend, more and more families might choose high-density urban living close to their work, if this were combined with a second home in more rural surroundings.[74] These are all questions that deserve further research.

LOCAL AND DISPERSED COMMUNITIES

Now to the implications of the geographical dispersal of leisure activities and social networks. For most people, these no longer bear any relationship to local authority boundaries. Some of the activities and networks spread across the nation and the world. But for most of the population, most of the time, the urban region is the meaningful setting.

The conclusion is surely that we need to order and plan the environment and the pattern of communications on a regional basis, the central idea being that the region could satisfy most of the day-to-day or week-to-week needs of its residents, and that public and private transport should be planned and organized so as to facilitate this. The regional transport networks should include not only links from peripheral communities into the centre but across the region as well.

Examples of the facilities with a regional catchment are further education, theatres, art cinemas, concert halls, exotic restaurants, top-level football grounds and competition swimming pools. There will, of course, be needs that people living in a region could meet only by going further afield—to London for the Covent Garden Opera or Scotland for a ski-ing holiday in the Highlands, to New York for a conference or the Riviera for sun. And there will naturally be inter-regional lines of communication—national motorways, railways and air routes, linking up with international routes.

Within the regional communication networks, however, there will still be a function for local community. Local social relationships are important to many people,[75] as suggested earlier, and people do after all depend on local shops, schools, etc. The planning task is to create a neighbourhood structure to meet these functional and psychological needs without such a marked separation of different localities as characterized the first new towns.

OUTSTANDING QUESTIONS

This paper suggested at the outset that what had happened in the past could help in looking ahead to the future. In trying to make some forecasts about changes in the social framework, this is the main approach that has been used—existing trends have been extrapolated, with modification where this seemed appropriate. The method has of course its limitations and a good many questions remain obscure.

It is not just that technology may surprise us all, that some innovations may change social life much more radically than has been suggested here. It is also that, though in a general way 'Tocqueville's Law' has proved reasonably useful, we do not really understand much about it. We do not know how diffusion works, what aspects of the lives of the 'few' will in fact prove attractive to the 'many' or which 'few' (i.e. the 'top' minorities in income, education or occupation) will provide the models for which sorts of taste or behaviour. Nor do we know in what conditions diffusion may operate 'upwards' instead of 'downwards' or 'vertically' (e.g. in terms of age) instead of 'horizontally'. We can make guesses, as this paper has done, but they may prove wrong.

The bigger underlying question is the one raised in the first paragraphs of the paper. This is the paradox about the class structure—how far can the process of 'merging', of increasing cultural homogeneity, go while the fundamental differences remain apparently unchanging? Above all, to echo the questions posed earlier, what will happen to poverty, colour and 'relative deprivation' in the emerging society? Again, further research is needed.

In particular, the older and poorer urban areas certainly pose planning problems. The environment of the future must provide not only for the affluent car-owning suburbanites but also for the minorities of income and colour, who at present live mainly in the older areas. What happens in these older areas clearly affects the city as a whole. As the rush to the suburbs continues, a social 'polarization' seems to be taking place inside the cities, though we do not have clear evidence about what is happening to the social composition of different types of residential areas. The inner urban areas seem to contain the poor and the very rich, while the rest live outside.[76] The process has gone even further in the United States, where divisions by colour and geography are all-important.[77] It could obviously happen in Britain too.

At present the impression is that some of the older central areas are deteriorating, physically and socially, much faster than they are being renewed. A co-ordinated attack, combining physical renewal and rehabilitation with the kind of 'positive discrimination' envisaged in the Plowden Report and in the Government's 'Urban Programme', is needed in the Brixtons and Notting Hills and in a different form in the Bethnal Greens and Bermondseys.

It would be tempting, in looking to the future, to concentrate resources upon new transport networks, better-planned new settlements, regional parks and the like. The older areas, particularly the poorest, plainly need attention as well. To strike the right balance between preparing for tomorrow and dealing with the inheritance from yesterday will not be easy, but it must be done. Thus, as well as social research on such topics as differences in the class structure, 'relative deprivation', life-styles, diffusion and suburbanization, there needs to be detailed investigation of the poorer urban areas, so as to suggest the appropriate combination of social and planning policies.

References

1. Apart from the help of fellow members of the DPU Group and its advisors, I am also indebted to my colleagues at the Institute of Community Studies, particularly Richard Mills, Michael Young and Sheila Yeatman. Useful comments on earlier drafts of the paper were made by Herbert Gans, David Grove and Phyllis Willmott.

2. In *Britain Revisited* (Gollancz, 1961) Tom Harrisson describes his impression, in comparing the Bolton of 1960 with that of 1936, of how much 'unchange' was mixed with 'change', pp. 25–45.

3. Guy Routh, *Occupation and Pay in Great Britain 1906–1960*, Cambridge University Press, 1965; see especially Table 1, pp. 4–5.

4. *Occupational Changes 1951–1961*, Manpower Studies No. 6, HMSO, 1967.

5. The American experience so far seems to suggest that the likely effects of automation have been exaggerated. See Daniel Bell in 'Towards the Year 2000: Work in Progress', *Daedalus*, Summer 1967, p. 676, particularly the reference to the President's Commission on Technology, Automation and Economic Progress.

6. D. V. Glass (Ed.), *Social Mobility in Britain*, Routledge, 1954.

7. Ibid., p. 188.

8. S. M. Lipset and R. Bendix, *Social Mobility in Industrial Society*, Heinemann, 1959, pp. 33–38.

9. P. M. Blau and O. D. Duncan, *The American Occupational Structure*, John Wiley, 1967, p. 424.

10. P. R. Kaim-Caudle, 'Selectivity and the Social Services', *Lloyds Bank Review*, April 1969, pp. 28–29.

11. *Higher Education*, HMSO, 1963, Appendix I, p. 54.

12. J. E. Meade, *Efficiency, Equality and the Ownership of Property*, Allen & Unwin, 1964, p. 27.

13. Guy Routh, op. cit., Chapter II.

14. J. L. Nicholson, *Redistribution of Income in the United Kingdom in 1959, 1957 and 1963*, Bowes & Bowes, 1964. See also John Hughes, 'The Increase in Inequality', *New Statesman*, 8 November 1968.

15. Richard M. Titmuss, *Income Distribution and Social Change*, Allen & Unwin, 1962, Chapter 8.

16. W. G. Runciman, reviewing changes in class, status and power in Britain from 1918 to 1962 concluded that 'inequality of status (i.e. prestige) was diminishing'. *Relative Deprivation and Social Justice*, Routledge, 1966, p. 118.

17. T. H. Marshall, *Citizenship and Social Class*, Cambridge University Press, 1950, Chapter I.

18. Mark Abrams, 'Consumption in the Year 2000', in Michael Young (Ed.), *Forecasting and the Social Sciences*, Heinemann, 1968, p. 37.

19. Meade, op. cit.; see also Hughes, op. cit.

20. Abrams, op. cit., p. 38.

21. D. C. Rowe, 'Private Consumption', in W. Beckerman, *et al.*, *The British Economy in 1975*, Cambridge University Press, 1965, p. 180.

22. David Donnison, *The Government of Housing*, Penguin, 1967, p. 194.

23. Quoted from Alexis de Tocqueville, *Democracy in America* by Daniel Bell in 'Towards the Year 2000: Work in Progress', p. 643 and p. 937.

24. John Burnett, *Plenty and Want: A Social History of Diet in England from 1815 to the Present Day*, Penguin, 1968, p. 16.

25. See D. Elliston Allen, *British Tastes*, Hutchinson, 1968.

26. See, for example, H. H. Gerth and C. Wright Mills (Eds), *From Max Weber: Essays in Sociology*, Routledge, 1948, p. 187.

27. John H. Goldthorpe, David Lockwood, Frank Bechhover and Jennifer Platt, 'The Affluent Worker and the Thesis of Embourgeoisement: Some Preliminary Research Findings', *Sociology*, Vol. 1 No. 1, January 1967. See also their *The Affluent Worker: Industrial Attitudes and Behaviour*, Cambridge University Press, 1968; *The Affluent Worker: Political Attitudes and Behaviour*, Cambridge University Press, 1968.

28. R. Dubin, 'Industrial Workers' Worlds', *Social Problems*, Vol. 3, No. 3, January 1956, pp. 131–42.

29. See Goldthorpe *et al.*, 'The Affluent Worker and the Thesis of Embourgeoisement', pp. 19–20.

30. Goldthorpe *et al.*, *The Affluent Worker: Political Attitudes and Behaviour*, pp. 11–19.

31. See, for example, David Reisman 'Leisure and Work in Post-Industrial Society', in Eric Larrabee and Rolf Meyersohn (Eds), *Mass Leisure*, Free Press, 1958.

32. Among recent British studies, see Hilda Jennings, *Societies in the Making* (Bristol), Routledge, 1962; C. Rosser and C. Harris, *The Family and Social Change* (Swansea), Routledge, 1965; Goldthorpe *et al.*, op. cit. See also, among American studies showing the role of kin and neighbours, Herbert J. Gans, *The Urban Villagers*, Free Press, 1962; M. B. Sussman, 'The Isolated Nuclear Family—Fact or Fiction?', in *Selected Studies in Marriage and the Family*, R. F. Winch, R. McGinnis and H. R. Barringer (Eds), Holt, Rinehart & Winston, 1962; M. Axelrod 'Urban Structure and Social Participation', in *Cities and Society*, P. K. Hatt and A. J. Reiss (Eds), Free Press, 1963.

33. Bennett M. Berger, *Working Class Suburb*, University of California Press, 1960; Peter Willmott, *The Evolution of a Community* (Dagenham), Routledge, 1963; Herbert J. Gans, *The Levittowners*, Allen Lane, The Penguin Press, 1967.

34. Goldthorpe *et al.*, 'The Affluent Worker and the Thesis of Embourgeoisement', pp. 22–23.

35. Peter Willmott and Michael Young, *Family and Class in a London Suburb*, Routledge, 1960, p. 122.

36. Goldthorpe *et al.*, *The Affluent Worker: Political Attitudes and Behaviour*, pp. 49–62.

37. Ibid., pp. 74–75. Also *Family and Class in a London Suburb*, op. cit., p. 115.

38. Runciman, op. cit., p. 192.

39. See William J. Goode, *World Revolution and Family Patterns*, Free Press, 1963; Dorothy R. Blisten, *The World of the Family*, Random House, 1963.

40. P. R. Cox, 'Marriage and Fertility Data of England and Wales', *Population Studies*, Vol. 5, November 1951, p. 140.

41. *Registrar General's Statistical Review for 1964, Part III, Commentary*, HMSO, 1967, p. 31.

42. Ibid., p. 17.

43. These calculations were kindly made by P. R. Cox.

44. This term itself could be criticized. Since, as noted earlier, more young people stay in education until a higher age, in one sense there is a contrary trend—children are economically dependent on their parents for longer than in the past. Even so, most are socially independent, or largely so, after about 15, and, as I argue later, this is likely to continue and to extend to residential independence.

45. Richard Titmuss, 'The Position of Women' in *Essays on the 'Welfare State'*, Allen & Unwin, 1958.

46. Quoted in S. R. Parker, *et al.*, *The Sociology of Industry*, Allen & Unwin, 1967, p. 50.

47. Colin M. Stewart, 'The Employment of Married Women in Great Britain', Paper to International Union for the Scientific Study of Population, London, 1969.

48. This pattern is described and discussed by Rhona Rapoport and Robert N. Rapoport 'The Dual-Career Family: A Variant Pattern and Social Change', *Human Relations*, Vol. 22, No. 1, February 1969, pp. 3–30.

49. Michael Young and Peter Willmott, *Family and Kinship in East London*, Routledge, 1957, pp. 6–15; F. Zweig, *The Worker in an Affluent Society*, Heinemann, 1961, pp. 30–32 and pp. 207–8; John and Elizabeth Newson, *Four Years Old in an Urban Community*, Allen & Unwin, 1968, pp. 522–4.

50. Charles Winick, 'The Beige Epoch: Depolarisation of Sex Roles in America', *The Annals of the American Academy of Political and Social Sciences*, Vol. 376, March 1968, pp. 18–24.

51. Mark Abrams, 'The Home-centred Society', *The Listener*, 26.11.59; Young and Willmott, *Family and Kinship in East London*, op. cit., p. 119 and pp. 127–36; Zweig, op. cit., pp. 206–9; Josephine Klein, *Samples from English Culture*, Routledge, 1965, Vol. 1, pp. 283–8.

52. Young and Willmott, *Family and Kinship in East London*, op. cit., Chapters I and X.

53. Willmott and Young, *Family and Class in a London Suburb*, op. cit., pp. 21–27.

54. Edmund Leach, *A Runaway World?*, BBC, 1968, pp. 42–46.

55. Rhona Rapoport and Robert N. Rapoport, op. cit.

56. Leach, op. cit., p. 45.

57. *The South East Study*, HMSO, 1964, p. 24.

58. *Registrar General's Statistical Review for 1962, Part III, Commentary*, HMSO, 1964, p. 50.

59. This kind of interpretation has been challenged in a recent article—Judith Blake, 'Are Babies Consumer Durables?', *Population Studies*, March 1968. See also a thorough discussion of the reasons for differential fertility, including hypotheses of this sort—Geoffrey Hawthorne and Joan Busfield, 'A Sociological Approach to British Fertility', in Julius Gould (Ed.), *Penguin Social Science Survey 1968*.

60. *New Society*, 14 December 1967, p. 847.

61. B. C. Roberts and J. L. Hirsch, 'Factors Influencing Hours of Work', in

B. C. Roberts and J. H. Smith (Eds), *Manpower Policy and Employment Trends*, London School of Economics and Political Science, 1966, pp. 111–13.

62. H. L. Wilensky, 'The Uneven Distribution of Leisure', *Social Problems*, Summer 1961, p. 39; this shows that half his (middle-class) sample worked 45 hours or more a week and one in five worked an average of eight hours or more at weekends.

63. H. Swados, 'Less Work: Less Leisure', in Larrabee and Meyershon (Eds), *Mass Leisure*, op. cit.

64. H. L. Wilensky, op. cit.

65. *Statistics on Incomes, Prices, Employment and Production*, September 1968, HMSO, p. 65.

66. Many of the senior civil servants, top managers, architects and doctors who work a 50- or 60-hour week have a complete break of a month or more each summer.

67. At present about 5 per cent of households in Britain own second homes or caravans, according to the BTA/Keele survey of leisure (British Travel Association/University of Keele, *Pilot National Recreation Survey, Report No. 1*, 1967, pp. 21–22). But rapid increases are reported in particular areas and in some villages (Blakeney, Norfolk, is one example) the second homes account for as many as a third of all dwellings.

68. Quoted in Mark Abrams, 'Britain: The Next 15 Years', *New Society*, 7 November 1968.

69. H. B. Rodgers, 'Leisure and Recreation', *Urban Studies*, Vol. 6, No. 3, November 1969, pp. 368–84.

70. Melvin M. Webber, 'The Urban Place and the Non-Place Urban Realm' in Melvin M. Webber *et al.*, *Explorations into Urban Structure*, University of Pennsylvania, 1963; and Melvin M. Webber 'Order in Diversity: Community without Propinquity', in Lowdon Wingo Jnr. (Ed.), *Cities and Space*, Johns Hopkins, 1964.

71. Herbert J. Gans, *The Levittowners*, op. cit.

72. Peter Willmott, 'East Kilbride and Stevenage', *Town Planning Review*, January, 1964, pp. 310–11; Hilda Jennings, op. cit., pp. 145–6; London County Council, *Survey into Design Aspects of Expanding Towns at Huntingdon, Haverhill and Thetford*, LCC, 10 January 1964, p. 2.

73. Herbert J. Gans, *The Levittowners*, op. cit., p. 222 and p. 246.

74. This possibility has been suggested by David Grove: 'Physical Planning and Social Change', *Forecasting and the Social Sciences*, op. cit., pp. 93–94.

75. See Peter Willmott, 'Social Research and New Communities', *AIP Journal*, November 1967.

76. See Ruth Glass's discussion of the process of 'gentrification', by which middle-class owner-occupiers are displacing working-class residents: Ruth Glass, 'Introduction', in Centre for Urban Studies, *London: Aspects of Change*, MacGibbon & Kee, 1964, pp. xviii–xix.

77. See Ruth Glass, op. cit.: '. . . the impression remains—and often it is the dominant one—that there is increasing segmentation' (p. xxii).

Chapter 6

Population Changes and their Educational Consequences

(Extract from the Crowther Report *15 to 18*, HMSO, 1959, pages 28–35.)

Men and women live longer and marry earlier than they used to, but they have smaller families. More married women have paid employment. All this is, of course, a matter of general knowledge: the purpose of this chapter is to give some indication of what the consequences of these facts have been, and ought to be, for education. What is taught in schools cannot, at least directly or quickly, influence these general social changes; but they profoundly affect what can and needs to be done in schools. It is in their context that we must plan.

EARLIER MARRIAGE AND SMALLER FAMILIES

People live longer. A hundred years ago only about one-third of the children born could expect to live to 65, while less than half of those who reached the age of 15 were still alive at 65. Now two-thirds of the children born, and three-quarters of those reaching the age of 15, may expect to be alive at 65. The improvement has been continuous. In the last half-century, between 1906 and 1956, the expectation of life at birth for men has risen from 48·5 years to 67·8 and for women from 52·4 years to 73·3. But beyond 65 there has been little change for over a century in the expectation of life. A man reaching 65 today may expect to live only one year longer than his great-grandfather a hundred years ago (for women the comparative figure is three years). The contemporary problem of old age is caused not by the elderly living longer, but by more people surviving to become elderly. Men and women aged 65 and over were only 5 per cent of the population in 1871 and 1901, by 1931 they had become 7 per cent, and by 1951 11 per cent. The proportion is still rising.

Men and women marry earlier—women markedly so. Unlike the increasing expectation of life, this has not been a continuous process but a swinging pendulum. From 1871 to 1911 the proportions of men and women marrying early steadily dropped. From 1911 to 1951 they have risen, slowly at first but latterly with a velocity that has carried them well above the 1871 level. This is shown in Table 1.

120

The changes are much more marked for women than for men. Today half the women in the country (and a quarter of the men) are married before they are 25. This compares with a third (and nearly a quarter of the men) at the previous peak ninety years ago. The trend towards early marriage has continued since the 1951 census. Over 4 per cent of the girls with whom this report is concerned are married women.

Table 1   *Proportions per Thousand Men and Women of Age-groups 15–19 and 20–24 who were or had been Married (Census Dates; England and Wales).*

Age-Group		1851	1861	1871	1881	1891
15–19	Men	4	5	5	5	4
	Women	25	30	32	25	19
20–24	Men	200	223	230	221	193
	Women	308	331	343	331	296

Age-Group		1901	1911	1921	1931	1941	1951
15–19	Men	3	2	4	3		5
	Women	15	12	18	18	No	44
20–24	Men	173	143	178	139	Census	238
	Women	272	243	274	258		482

Families are smaller. The decline in the number of births per family has been a continuous process for over a hundred years. The average number of children born to a woman marrying in mid-Victorian times has been estimated to have been 5·8; for women married in 1925 it was 2·2. The Royal Commission on Population estimated that about 9 per cent of marriages taking place about 1860 were childless compared with 17 per cent of those taking place in 1925. Of the 1860 marriages, 5 per cent produced one child only; 6 per cent, two; 8 per cent, three; and 72 per cent, more than three children. The corresponding figures for the 1925 marriages were 25 per cent with one child, 25 per cent with two, 14 per cent with three children and 19 per cent with more than three. At first the fall in size of families was much more marked in the professional classes, but this contrast has grown less, primarily through a reduction in the size of families of manual workers, but to some extent also by a tendency to slightly larger families than a generation ago in the professional classes. We have no firm data of recent years about the distribution of family size, but the 1951 census provides details for each social class of the size of private households and of the number of children under 16 that they contained, which is close enough to the same thing to serve as a rough guide. (It should be explained that a retired person living alone, and an establishment in which parents and children, relations and domestic staff live together, both equally constitute a single household.) The remarkable thing is that the size of households, and the number of children under 16 they contain, vary very little class by class from the average of all classes, though social classes 4 and 5 still contain a rather higher proportion of households with 3 or more children. Broadly speaking, however, we may say that, in every class, over half the households had no children at home on the day the 1951 census was taken, that getting on for a quarter had one child, about one-seventh had two children and one-twelfth had three or more.

More married women are engaged in paid work. The 1901 census classified just under one-third of all women (32 per cent) as 'gainfully occupied'; the 1951 census just over one-third (35 per cent). The proportion of married women who were 'gainfully occupied' rose from 13 per cent in 1901 to 23 per cent in 1951. In 1901 22 per cent of the women who were 'gainfully occupied' were married; in 1951 the percentage was 40. Quite as significant is the change in the nature of women's occupations. In 1901 four of every five women employed were either in domestic service occupations (including laundry work), or in the manufacture and sale either of textile fabrics and dresses or of food, drink and tobacco. Even so, the range of occupations followed by women was considerably more diversified then than it had been twenty years before. The process of diversification has gone steadily on, and there have been large increases in the last twenty years in the numbers and proportions following occupations which require some education above the minimum. The greatest single increase, both proportionately (122 per cent) and absolutely (700,000), was among clerks and typists. The increase in the professional and technical occupations (which included nursing and all the medical services, as well as teaching and social work) was 35 per cent; but even so the ratio of women to men in this whole group was lower in 1951 than in 1931.

SMALLER FAMILIES, LONGER EDUCATION

These radical changes in the structure and way of life of the population have had, and will continue to have, many repercussions on the educational system. We choose six which seem to us of special consequence in their bearing on our terms of reference. Three of these have a direct connection with the organization and content of education. They are: the greater ability of the individual family to support a lengthy education for its children; the greater freedom of the married woman to take up paid employment; the fact that, for the increasing number of girls, marriage now follows hard on, or even precedes, the end of education. The other three are more concerned with the nature of the society in which children grow up. They are: the larger proportion of old people which society as a whole has to support; the fact that the family group covers a much smaller age-range than previously, thus limiting a boy's or girl's intimate circle (apart from parents) to his or her own precise contemporaries; and the fact that both births and deaths are now rare events in most children's lives.

It seems clear that most families can now support a longer school education for their children than used to be the case. Families are, as we have seen, smaller in all social groups. They are started earlier in life; and, as the Royal Commission on Population pointed out, about four-fifths of all the children who will be born to a group of married couples are born in the first ten years of married life. These facts taken together seem to us significant. Lack of money used to make it necessary in the days of large families for manual workers to put their children to work as early as possible. The father reached his peak earning capacity in early manhood; each additional child meant an increased cost on a fixed income until the older children could go to work to relieve, and contribute to, the family exchequer. The younger children in a large family, moreover, might still be dependent as the parents approached the time when their earning capacity would grow less or disappear. To this economic force working against any longer education than the unavoidable minimum may probably be added a psychological one. Younger children obviously need attention, and nearly always receive it. Older children may need it just as much, but their need is not so apparent. They are more likely to get it when there are no younger ones to distract the parents' notice. It is a tribute to the courage and the conviction of their parents that many boys and girls from the homes of manual workers did in the past get a secondary education or better; but the number of them was necessarily small. It was not until the days of generally small families that manual workers and their wives could reasonably be expected to look at education for their children in the same sort of perspective as non-manual workers. The manual worker of today normally has a family whose numbers do not constitute an excessive burden on his income, and whose members may all be expected to be grown up and independent, however long the education he gives them, before he retires on pension. Moreover, his wife

123

is very likely to be able to supplement the family income when the children are older. This diagnosis is corroborated by the fact that children in large families tend to have a shorter education than those in small families. Among National Service recruits to the Army and the RAF the proportion who had left school at 15 rises with each additional member of the family from which they come, from 58 per cent among only children, to 61, 71, 80, 86 and 92 per cent in families with six or more children. And this pattern is repeated in each occupation group. (Further statistics are contained in Volume II of the Crowther Report.) With the exception of these large families, then, we can today for the first time say that the family situation of all classes is such as to put no barriers in the way of longer education. But the exception remains. In recent years, society has made some provision towards the cost of supporting a large family through family allowances, income tax allowances and, for those with really low incomes, through maintenance allowances, but the provision is hardly sufficient as yet to give equality of opportunity to members of large families.

WOMEN'S EDUCATION FOR MARRIAGE AND EMPLOYMENT

The reduction in family size, the earlier age of marriage, the earlier incidence of child-bearing inside marriage, longer life and better health—all these are making it increasingly possible for marriage to mark not the end, but simply a break in a woman's career. Indeed it is no longer marriage itself, but child-bearing and child-care which today signal a withdrawal from outside employment. How long a withdrawal? There is a period when part-time employment is possible, but not full-time. But when full allowance has been made for this, for any slight increase in family size, and for the years of retirement, it remains true that the wife of today has a large number of years which she can devote to activities outside her home (whether 'gainful' or voluntary), and that the changed outlook of today makes her want to use them in this way. This desire is in line with the economic and social needs of the community; it does not, however, fit in well either with the organization and conditions of employment, or, in some respects, with the education provided for girls in secondary schools. The Royal Commission on Population (Cmd. 7695, HMSO, 1949, p. 160) pointed out that:

> There is often a real conflict between motherhood and a whole-time 'career'. Part of this conflict is inherent in the biological function of women, but part of it is artificial and the persistence of this artificial element tends to depress the status of motherhood into that of an inferior alternative to outside employment or

public life. We, therefore, welcome the removal of the marriage bar in such employment as teaching and the civil service and we think that a deliberate effort should be made to devise adjustments that would render it easier for women to combine motherhood and the care of a home with outside activities.

The conclusion to which this leads is twofold. In the first place, attention must be paid (as the Royal Commission suggested) to the re-organization of those professions and occupations which do (or might) employ women so as to enable married women to play their part in them, or to resume it when the period of pregnancy and infant care is over. Education authorities are in an especially responsible position in this regard insofar as married women are urgently needed as teachers, and teaching is a profession in which women are employed alongside men. It is increasingly important to solve the problem of the exodus of married women from teaching. Secondly, girls should be encouraged to qualify before marriage in a greater number of professions or occupations which will provide opportunities for them in later years. Teaching, social work, the health services, the clothing trades and commerce are the occupations usually thought of when the school curriculum is planned, but experience in this and other countries suggests that there are other occupations which can be combined with marriage or in which a married woman can bring herself up to date after a few years' absence from work by a relatively brief refresher course.

The earlier age at which women now marry has serious consequences for the education of adolescent girls. It hardly leaves time for a girl to become fully qualified professionally, and to gain experience in the exercise of her skill, before marriage and childbirth interrupt her career. It will, we think, be generally agreed that some period of independence, of being out in the world, before marriage is highly desirable. It is increasingly difficult to reconcile this with the demands of school life. Certainly it points to a radically new conception of the way in which girls of 17 and 18 should be treated. If they are to remain in full-time education it will, we think, be necessary to treat them far more as students than as schoolgirls. Some schools are, we know, aware of the problem but they are not yet the majority. It is not only, though this is important, that girls will not stay at school if they feel that they are being treated as children and are identifiable by the general public as schoolgirls on irrelevant occasions. We are even more concerned that they should learn to behave and to react as adults. It is not calf love, but the love which leads to marriage that they feel. Where the intellectually abler girls are concerned, it is difficult for the schools to adjust to this sharpening contrast between career interests and personal demands, for most of what they learn in school is related to their professional training and to entrance into the universities and other institutions where it is pursued. There is not much scope—in school hours, at least—for giving them any education specifically related to their special interests as women.

With the less able girls, however, we think that the schools can and should make more adjustments (more than all but a handful have yet done) to the fact that marriage now looms much larger and nearer in the pupils' eyes than it has ever done before. Their needs are much more sharply differentiated from those of boys of the same age than is true of the academically abler groups. Nearly nine times as many girls as boys get married before they are 19. This is reflected in the immediate interests of the boys and girls in the last year or two of the school course. There can be no doubt that at this stage boys' thoughts turn most often to a career, and only secondly to marriage and the family; and that the converse obtains with girls. It is plain, then, that, if it is sound educational policy to take account of natural interests, there is a clear case for a curriculum which respects the different roles they play. While the ultimate objective should be to help both boys and girls to grow up as intelligent and responsible citizens, the proximate objective should take the interests they display during this phase of their lives into consideration.

At this time, therefore, the prospect of courtship and marriage should rightly influence the education of the adolescent girl. Though the general objectives of secondary education remain unchanged, her direct interest in dress, personal appearance and in problems of human relations should be given a central place in her education. The greater psychological and social maturity of girls makes such subjects acceptable—and socially necessary. Girls must be treated even more completely than adolescent boys, as young adults. It is the extension of education to older pupils, as well as the increasingly early sophistication of girls which have not only made this differentiation necessary, but have also given the subjects we have mentioned their strong emotional charge. The increase in the number of early marriages is, in any case, creating a problem for the schools; it will be more serious when the school-leaving age is raised.

THE OLD AND THE YOUNG

The fact that the elderly and retired now form a higher proportion of the whole population than in the past, and that the proportion is still rising, has important educational consequences. It is certain that we can support them and increase the standard of living of the whole community only if there is increased efficiency in production and distribution at all levels. And increased efficiency means both better education and longer education. But there is another educational consequence, quite as serious in its implications, of the ageing population. Are the old to be regarded as a burden—an unwelcome by-product of the efficiency of the welfare state—or are they to have a highly regarded place in society? The problem is not only an economic one, but a moral one—in both aspects it has a bearing on education.

There remain the two less tangible, but no less important, influences of population changes on education—the disappearance of death, and indeed of birth, as a common incident of growing up in a family, and the disappearance of the 'all-through' family which bridged the generations, to borrow a metaphor from the title of those older schools which cater for all ages from 5 to 15. Death, in fact, in the experience of most children is limited to the death of the old, whereas not so long ago it was realized as something that might strike anyone at any time. Throughout the whole of the last half of the nineteenth century the infant mortality rate was of the order of 150 per thousand live births; in this century it has steadily and dramatically fallen—to 63 in the period 1930–1932 and to 30 in 1951. Ninety years ago half the male deaths were those of boys and men under 20; by 1951 the proportion had dropped to 6 per cent. The great majority were of men over 45. Fifty to a hundred years ago boys and girls were frequently reminded that they were, so to speak, tenants-at-will of life, not freeholders. Today they have—mercifully—a much greater sense of personal security, but this may well make the shock of corporate insecurity all the greater when in their teens they first become consciously aware of the fundamental political anxieties of our time. The old 'all-through' family, though it had its disadvantages, especially in curtailing education, acted as a school for personal responsibility and informal social education. No one child could long hold the centre of the stage. Parents had younger children to occupy their attention as the older ones grew up. There was a constant succession of new roles to be played by the various members of the family circle as its numbers grew and its composition gradually changed. The generations merged into one another. In the characteristic household of today there is no change in the composition of the family, once established, until it suddenly disrupts some sixteen to twenty years later. The new family pattern, and it is new not only in relation to the recent past but to all recorded history, tends to emphasize and increase the inherent isolation and self-centredness of the adolescent.

127

Chapter 7

Poverty Rediscovered

ADRIAN SINFIELD

The reluctant 'rediscovery' of the poor has, over the last decade, begun in most of the industrialized countries of Europe and North America (Sinfield, 1967b). The implications of this persistence of economic and social inequality seem to be particularly relevant to the study of minority groups in Britain, yet so far there is little evidence that this has been recognized. This article discusses the current state of our knowledge about the poor and relates this to what is probably the most widely-held view among the non-poor about the causes of poverty. Finally, I want to add a brief personal comment on the relevance of this to the study of race.

THE CONCEPT OF POVERTY

Who the poor are found to be obviously depends upon the definition of poverty employed. The subsistence approach first used by Seebohm Rowntree in his 1899 survey of York (1901) has been criticized by Peter Townsend in particular, who has shown that the costing of 'necessities' needed by households of different size and structure to maintain their minimum efficiency does not provide a scientific and objective poverty-line. The notion of subsistence depends on the definition of 'needs' and these can only be specified in reference to the current standards of living in the community—and such standards, of course, change over time (Townsend, 1962a). The poor, therefore, are those 'individuals and families whose resources, over time, fall seriously short of the resources commanded by the average individual or family in the community in which they live' (Townsend, 1962a, p. 225). Poverty, then, is a relative and dynamic concept closely related to the issues of inequality and redistribution which have been discussed in particular in the work of Richard Titmuss (1958, 1962, 1965).

THE EXTENT OF POVERTY IN BRITAIN TODAY

The only evidence of the extent of poverty in Britain derives from secondary analyses of data from the Ministry of Labour Household Expenditure Surveys. In the most detailed study Brian Abel-Smith

128

and Peter Townsend (1965) took as the cut-off point for poverty the amount to which each household would be entitled to according to the then National Assistance scales of payment (determined basically by the number and age of a man's dependants plus the actual rent paid), plus 40 per cent of the scale rate. Since in practice some assistance payments were made above the basic rates and in others certain types of income were 'disregarded' in assessing payments, national assistance plus 40 per cent was estimated to approximate most closely to the average standard of living of most recipients (Townsend, 1962a, p. 214). This, it was argued, might be regarded as the 'official' poverty line.

By this criteria one person in every seven—some seven-and-a-half million people—lived in poverty in the United Kingdom in 1960, somewhat more than in 1953–4. One person in every twenty-five— some two million—lived in what might be called extreme poverty, at or below the basic assistance level. The largest group in poverty in 1960 were three million people living in households where the head was in full-time work—one million of these in extreme poverty. Two-and-a-half million were people of pensionable age (65 for men and 60 for women)—850,000 in extreme poverty. Three-quarters of a million lived in what are now called 'fatherless' families—300,000 in extreme poverty. Nearly another three-quarters of a million were in households where one parent, not necessarily the head—had been disabled or sick for three months or more—some 250,000 in extreme poverty. Finally, half a million lived in households where the father was unemployed—250,000 in extreme poverty.

THE OLD

Of these groups the most investigated are the old. Local (Townsend, 1963), national (Cole and Utting, 1962; National Assistance Board, 1966) and now cross-national (Shanas *et al.*, 1968; with data on Britain alone, Townsend, 1967c) studies have shown the severe economic impact of retirement, and the inadequacy of state insurance pensions in preventing deprivation for retired manual workers in particular. The plight of the very old and women living alone is particularly acute, and if it were not for the aid from family and friends, the hardship of many in old age would be even greater (Cole and Utting, 1962, p. 103).

Research into the living-standards of the old has been closely linked with the debate about their place in an urban industrial society. Though the studies, particularly the cross-national, have shown that the integration of the old into the community is greater

129

than often assumed, there is evidence that certain minorities are both deprived and isolated (Tunstall, 1966). The segregation and poverty of many in old people's homes have also been vividly described and analysed (Townsend, 1962b).

THE SICK AND DISABLED

There have only been a few small studies of the economic situation of the sick and disabled (Bowerbank, 1958; Shaw, 1958; Townsend, 1967b; Veit-Wilson, 1967; Willmott, 1963). For this group, too, poverty and social segregation are associated. In general 'society tends to give weak support to the principles of economic independence and social integration or participation' which the disabled themselves wanted and 'fairly strong support, some of it unwitting, to the enforced dependence and social segregation of the disabled' which they resented and did not want (Townsend, 1967b, p. 3).

LARGE FAMILIES

About four times as great a proportion of large as small families have been found in poverty (Abel-Smith and Townsend, 1965; Ministry of Social Security, 1967), but there has only been one detailed study, of eighty-six London families with five or more dependent children (Land, 1970). Families' reluctance to admit their poverty and the lack of adequate information led to considerable underutilization of the existing social services—a finding later confirmed by the government's own survey of families with at least two children (Ministry of Social Security, 1967, pp. 24–9). In view of the belief widely current that the majority of the poor are in large families (and the conclusions about the responsibility of these that many draw), it should be pointed out that many more children in poverty live in families with only two dependent children than in families with six children and more (Ministry of Social Security, 1967).

FATHERLESS FAMILIES

The few studies of families without resident fathers have emphasized the significance of society's values in influencing differential treatment of the fatherless which adds to the lack of the male wage-earner the absence of adequate resources. Financially, war widows are better off, then industrial widows, then 'civilian widows', although the needs of the family are unchanged (Marris, 1958). The linking of social honour and economic resources extends even further: widows as a whole are best off, then the divorced, and the separated, then the

130

abandoned and finally the unmarried mothers. In one study not only were these last the most stigmatized, they seemed likely to receive least help. The lack of sympathy and of resources only accentuated their isolation from society and so made them particularly dependent on the support of casual relationships (Marsden, 1969).

THE UNEMPLOYED

The relatively low level of unemployment since the war has led to a neglect of the problems of those who are unemployed. There appears to be little economic hardship among redundant workers where the local demand for labour has been high, although in other areas there has been longer unemployment and economic sacrifice, especially among older and disabled workers (Wedderburn, 1965; House and Knight, 1967; Knight, 1968). But the redundant are probably not typical: an official survey showed that over two-thirds of men unemployed in October 1964 had been out of work at least once before in the previous four years (Ministry of Labour, 1966). A random sample of unemployed in the North-east in 1963–4 had experienced considerable recurrent unemployment (quarter of the past five years 'on the dole') and many families, especially those with children to support, lived in or close to poverty whether the wage-earner had a job or not. The unskilled, the disabled and older workers were most heavily disadvantaged in finding work and the existing services provided little aid (Sinfield, 1967a).

'WORKING BUT POOR'

The most surprising finding in Abel-Smith and Townsend's study (1965) was that the largest group of the poor lived in households headed by a full-time wage-earner and the significance of this has yet to be fully realized. Beveridge and the other planners of the 1940s believed that it was the responsibility of society to look after those for whom the free market did not work—the unemployed, the sick, the industrially injured and those who were retired. They seem to have made the implicit assumption that wages from employment would take care of the rest, once Family Allowances had been provided for those with children to support. This assumption is now in urgent need of questioning and the wage system, the allocation of economic resources through work, needs to be more closely examined. In fact it is the poor in work we know least about (although see Little, 1966; Marquand, 1967; Robinson, 1967; Edmonds and Radice, 1968).

131

Many are probably disabled or in poor health and unable to work the long shifts of overtime that make a wage tolerable: many probably come from those whose work is subject to frequent periods of unemployment, but we do not know what proportion of the poor in work these form. In 1960—in the Ministry of Labour survey on the distribution of earnings (1961)—one man in ten earned less than the assistance level for a man, wife and three children with an average council-house rent, at that time £10. Up to 1966 average earnings in most low paid industries had risen less quickly than in other industries (Townsend, 1967a). Altogether one-quarter of the employed-poor worked in central or local government

In fact there appears to have been very little change in occupational differentials in earnings since before the First World War (Routh, 1965). There was no change at all in the relation of wages of unskilled men to average national earnings between 1913 and 1960 and there was little evidence of a reduction in the differential between rich and poor occupations.

POVERTY AND THE LIFE CYCLE

Although knowledge about these different categories of the poor, particularly the aged, is increasing, scarcely anything is known about the relationship between the groups isolated in discussion and research. The categories described above are not, of course, mutually exclusive but it is not known how they overlap at any one time *or* over a lifetime. In fact, a large proportion of the population seems likely to be in poverty once or more in the course of their lives while a much smaller group may be in poverty for most of their lives. The poor do not at present constitute a separate entity or class in Britain. Although because of its generally lower earnings, the working-class is, of course, more vulnerable to poverty and for longer periods, there will be many middle-class poor for reasons of disability, illness or retirement—and a white-collar clerical job does not always ensure a wage above the poverty line.

THE LOCATION OF THE POOR

We have depressingly little evidence about the geographical concentration of the poor, although we know that there are marked regional inequalities: the average man in the south is better and longer educated, earns and saves more, is ill and unemployed less and lives longer than his counterpart in the north (Hammond, 1968). Certainly the data available suggest that rates of poverty are higher in the depressed regions mostly far from London than in the more prosperous areas of London, the South-East and the Midlands, and in remote rural areas or inner-city slums rather than surburban commuterland. The combination of these with the poverty-linked characteristics described earlier suggests that the chances of poverty would be very high among elderly widows living alone in the slums of Belfast and very low among the two-child family in a London suburb.

THE STRATEGY OF 'SPECIAL AREAS'

Recently there has been increasing support for special area programmes. The Plowden Committee, for example, has advocated educational priority areas (Central Advisory Council for Education (England) 1967, Vol. 1, Chapter 5), the Seebohm Committee priority areas for community development or social development areas (1968, paras. 485–90), the National Committee for Commonwealth Immigrants areas of special housing need (1967), and the Home Secretary has forecast help for areas of severe social deprivation (Callaghan, 1968). Some of the strategies envisaged are coming more and more to resemble the community action programmes in the American War on Poverty (Marris and Rein, 1967). Although there has so far been only one intensive study of a poor area—in Nottingham (Coates and Silburn, 1967)—rather than a poor group, the special area attack appears to be widely regarded as a strategy for tackling the problems of inequality in the distribution of resources and services.

In evaluating such programmes for combating poverty, the vital distinction between incidence and composition needs to be kept in mind. Those areas with the greatest incidence or risk of poverty do not necessarily (and are usually very unlikely to) contain a high proportion of the poor. Programmes, therefore, aimed at reducing the incidence of poverty in these areas may do little for, or even divert resources from, the majority of the poor, and may not significantly reduce the number in poverty in the whole country.

This seems to be very largely what has happened in the United States where poor and black are treated as synonymous by many administrators and the great majority of the American non-poor. The stereotypical poor is thought to be the Negro high-school dropout unemployed in the urban slum; whatever the value of the plethora of different programmes launched for or against this group in these areas, they have nothing to do with those poor who are at work, in school, sick, retired and living outside these areas, whether they be black or white.

An all-out attack on a number of specific areas is much more administratively attractive—certainly cheaper and potentially quicker—than the careful re-examination of the basic fabric of society that the knowledge we have of poverty appears to demand. Although specific programmes focused on the areas of greatest 'need' are of obvious importance as part of the planning to reduce poverty and inequality, they are not substitutes for such wider action.

THE 'CULTURE OF POVERTY'

The 'special areas' approach, unless it is closely and explicitly related to wider planning—and so far it has not been—seems certain to strengthen the growing support here for the popular versions of a 'culture of poverty' which has already become so notorious in the United States. Contrary, apparently, to Oscar Lewis' own intention (1966), the notion of a sub-culture of poverty has been used to explain poverty. People, it is argued, are poor because they lack adequate socialization or proper motivation to escape or break out from their circumstances. The policies generally derived from such hypotheses centre on changing the individual in some way—by training or retraining, education, social casework or therapy. Essentially, the structure of society itself is accepted—the poor merely need help in adapting to it.

This version of the culture of poverty gains great acceptance very largely because of the extent to which it supports the conventional wisdom of the non-poor and because it sanctions the existing social structure. Its acceptance is also speeded by the ease with which distinct groups can be defined as poor—for example, the coloured immigrant in the urban slum. Put very crudely—as it often has been put to me by many, including administrators, not only in Britain but in Europe and North America—this is simply a revamping of the old Horatio Alger and Samuel Smiles self-made man approach. A man can escape poverty if he really tries hard enough—unfortunately, the new version adds, he is held back by the culture of poverty.

Because of the strong support given to this thesis, it is important to underline its weaknesses. Quite apart from the flimsy empirical evidence supporting the thesis—a few families in different American countries—it can only really hope to explain why people remain poor when there are *opportunities* for escape. If the opportunities are not there, the motivation of the poor is not relevant, and if the poor are ill or retired and so outside the labour force, neither motivation nor opportunity is relevant.

134

In contrast, the findings of the research into poverty have under-lined the need to study poverty in its societal context as a relative lack of resources, intimately related to the issues of distribution and redistribution. The poverty of men and their families is still very largely determined by the rewards they can command for their labour in the market, for the 'normal' involvement or integration in society, and participation in its rewards, is through the labour market. Those, therefore, who are even more dependent on society because they are outside the labour force are especially vulnerable, both to poverty and isolation. This is not explained by the culture of poverty—if anything, this explains the culture.

PERSONAL POSTSCRIPT

Admittedly the study of poverty has much to learn from the study of race—in particular, perhaps, the extent to which the dominant group may determine the fortunes of minority groups—but at the same time research into poverty and inequality has given fresh emphasis to the importance of economic resources in controlling one's ability to take part in society and the significance of this has been neglected by others.

Many studies of race and coloured immigrants in this country seem, tacitly, to lend support to the notion of a culture of poverty. In general the data on resources collected in such surveys are usually pretty scanty and there has been a lack of studies comparing black and white residents in a community: as a result there appears a tendency to attribute to cultural causes what may be due to differing economic circumstances.

Let me put this even more bluntly. From many writers on racial inequality I gain the impression that there is relatively little aware-ness of the general situation of poverty and inequality in Britain. Sometimes the coloured immigrant and his family seem to be regarded as the only objects of discrimination—and this in a society still marked for its rigid class system. Words like 'segregation, inequality, prejudice' are used as if they could only refer to racial situations and not, as in this article, to many other groups in society. This seems to me to have two very real dangers. First, while in-equality is believed to affect *only* a small and easily identified group, support is given to middle-class views about increasing equality (Titmuss, 1962). This may well lead, as in the fifties, to a reduction in the attack on social and economic inequality and poverty (Runciman, 1966). Second, prejudice against 'blacks' may be attacked and weakened while prejudice against the lowest economic classes may be

135

further strengthened. Once again, the poor, both black and white, will be the losers.

ADDENDUM, 1972

In 1972 there is perhaps a greater awareness of the structural factors leading to and maintaining poverty in a still class-bound society. The sharp increase in unemployment has once again drawn attention to the economic causes of deprivation. The debate on the low-paid has gained a larger audience as the introduction of the Family Income Supplement and the general trend towards selectivity has intensified the problem of the 'poverty trap' (where real income drops as a rise in monetary income ends entitlement to means-tested services, benefits and rebates).

These developments have set discussions of poverty more firmly within the context of inequality and led to a focus on the different systems of distribution and redistribution, with a vigorous debate over the Labour Government's policies and their effect on poverty and inequality (Townsend and Bosanquet, 1962; Bull, 1971; Child Poverty Action Group, 1970). The changing demands of the occupational and industrial structure, combined with the increasing costs of participation in the urban system, have been shown to create a new process of pauperism; despite wage increases, real income has fallen because of swiftly rising housing costs as well as the general inflation (Pahl, 1971; also Goldthorpe, 1969). Housing and tax reform are currently the two most-discussed policy areas affecting the poor (Child Poverty Action Group, 1972).

There has not been the increasing flow of literature on the subject that one might have expected in 1968, although there is now more available on the low-paid (National Board for Prices and Incomes, 1971; Hughes in Bull, 1971 and Townsend and Bosanquet, 1972; Pahl, 1971; Bosanquet, 1971; Sinfield and Twine, 1969—and on the distribution of earnings in Department of Employment, 1970 and Lydall, 1968). The first reports on the special area programmes are about to be published (Halsey, 1972; for an assessment of the strategy, see Holman, 1970). The new publications have been added to the bibliography, but *The Poor and The Poorest* still provides the most detailed analysis, until the results of the first national study of the incidence of poverty and the distribution of resources in the United Kingdom are available (Townsend, 1973). A review in 1969 of the available evidence concluded that 'a significant minority of the population (between 4 per cent and 9 per cent) have incomes which are below . . . the "national minimum" defined by the Government through the Supplementary Benefit scale' (Atkinson, 1969, p. 96; see also Gough and Stark, 1968; Lafitte in Holman, 1970).

The nature of this poverty has been revealed in the accounts of the unemployed (Gould and Kenyon, 1972), in a meticulous documentation of institutional poverty for the mentally handicapped (Morris, 1969), and in a Government comparison of families on supplementary benefit which showed clearly the ways in which the rules of the supplementary benefit scheme restricted the incomes of the unemployed in particular, as well as indicating the general extent of deprivation (Department of Health and Social Security, 1972; see Bottomley, 1971, for the first of a series of reports on fourteen poor families in London).

Such findings direct the search for the causes of poverty away from the behaviour of the poor to that of the non-poor and to the allocation of resources throughout society. The fact that poverty had to be 'rediscovered' yet again poses important questions about our society. Its invisibility is no more a sufficient explanation today than it was in Manchester in 1844 (Engels, republished 1969, pp. 79–80). Closer examination of the rediscovery, the resistance to this and the breakthroughs, the means by which the neglect was sanctioned and legitimated, the important role of government and the professions in determining and limiting the issues brought before the rest of society may itself contribute to a better understanding of the forces maintaining poverty. It leads us to analyse the functions played by poverty in a modern industrial society and to consider the extent to which more powerful groups benefit from the persistence of inequalities.

Bibliography to Chapter 7

Abel-Smith, Brian and Townsend, Peter (1965), *The Poor and the Poorest*, Occasional Papers on Social Administration, No. 17, Bell.

Abel-Smith, Brian and Bagley, C. (1967), 'The Problem of Establishing Equivalent Standards of Living for Families of Different Composition', *International Seminar on Poverty*, University of Essex, published in Townsend (1970).

Atkinson, A. B. (1969), *Poverty in Britain and the Reform of Social Security*, University of Cambridge Press.

Bagley, Christopher (1968), *The Cost of a Child*, Institute of Psychiatry.

Behrend, Hilde and Knowles, A. 'What is Lower Pay?' *Social Science Research Council Newsletter*, No. 8, March 1970, pp. 19–21; and No. 12, June 1971, pp. 5–7.

Bosanquet, Nicholas (1971), 'Jobs and the Low-paid', *Poverty*, Child Poverty Action Group, No. 18, Spring.

Bosanquet, Nicholas and Stephens, R. J. (1972), 'Another Look at Low Pay', *Journal of Social Policy*, Vol. 1, No. 3, July.

Bottomley, Virginia (1971), *Families with Low Incomes in London*, Child Poverty Action Group pamphlet.

Bowerbank, M. (1958), 'Living on a State-maintained Income, II', *Case Conference*, Vol. 4, No. 10.

Bull, David (ed.) (1971), *Family Poverty*, Duckworth.

Callaghan, J. (1968), *Hansard*, 22 July, Col. 40.

Central Advisory Council for Education (England) (1967), *Children and their Primary Schools* (The Plowden Report), HMSO. (Discussed in 3 articles in *New Society*, 12 January 1967, pp. 46–50.)

Child Poverty Action Group (1970), *Poverty and the Labour Government*.

Child Poverty Action Group (1972), 'Housing and the Poor', *Poverty*, No. 22, Spring.

Coates, Ken and Silburn, Richard (1970), *Poverty: The Forgotten Englishmen*, Penguin. (An earlier version of part of the area study was published as *St. Ann's: Poverty, Deprivation and Morale in a Nottingham Community*, Nottingham University, Department of Adult Education, 1967.

Cole (Wedderburn) Dorothy and Utting, J. (1962), *The Economic Circumstances of Old People*, Occasional Papers on Social Administration, No. 4, Codicote Press, Welwyn.

Daniel, W. W. (1968), *Racial Discrimination in England*, Penguin, (based on the P.E.P. Report, *Racial Discrimination in Britain*, published in April 1967).

Davie, Ronald *et al.* (1972), *From Birth to Seven*, Longmans.

Edmonds, J. and Radice, G. (1968), *Low Pay*, Fabian Research Series No. 270, Fabian Society.

Elder, Glen H. Junr. (1965), 'Life Opportunity and Personality: Some Consequences of Stratified Education in Great Britain', *Sociology of Education*, Vol. 38, No. 3, Spring (reprinted by the Institute of International Studies, University of California, Berkeley).

Employment, Department of, (1970), *New Earnings Survey 1968*, HMSO. Repeated yearly since April 1970.

Engels, Friedrich (1892), *The Condition of the Working-Class in England in 1844*, Allen & Unwin, republished by Panther Books, 1969.

Franklin, N. N. (1967), 'The Concept and Measurement of Minimum Living Standards', *International Labour Review*, Vol. 96, pp. 271–298.

Galbraith, J. K. (1962), *The Affluent Society*, Penguin edition.

Glastonbury, Bryan (1971), *Homeless Near a Thousand Homes*, Allen & Unwin.

Goldthorpe, J. H. (1969), 'Social Inequality and Social Integration in Modern Britain', *Advancement of Science*, December, pp. 190–202.

Gough, I. and Stark, T. (1968), 'Low Incomes in the United Kingdom, 1954, 1959 and 1963', *Manchester School of Economic and Social Studies*, June, pp. 173–184.

Gould, Tony and Kenyon, Joe (1972), *Stories from the Dole Queue*, Temple Smith.

Greve, John; Page, Dilys; and Greve, Stella (1971), *Homelessness in London*, Chatto & Windus and Scottish Academic Press.

Halsey, A. H. (ed.) (1972), *Educational Priority*, HMSO (to be followed by reports on the individual areas).

Hammond, Edwin (1968), *An Analysis of Regional Economic and Social Statistics*, University of Durham Rowntree Research Unit.

Health and Social Security, Department of (1971), *Two-Parent Families*, HMSO.

Health and Social Security, Department of (1972), *Families Receiving Supplementary Benefit*, HMSO.

Holman, Robert (ed.) (1970), *Socially Deprived Families in Britain*, Bedford Square Press, National Council of Social Service.

House, J. W. and Knight, E. M. (1967), *Pit Closure and the Community: Report to the Ministry of Labour, Papers on Migration and Mobility in Northern England*, No. 5, Department of Geography, University of Newcastle, December.

Institute of Economic Affairs (1970), *Policy for Poverty: Report of an IEA Study Group*, IEA.

Isaacs, Bernard *et al.* (1972), *Survival of the Unfittest: A Study of Geriatric Patients in Glasgow*, Routledge.

Knight, E. M. (1968), *Men Leaving Mining, West Cumberland, 1966–67, Report to the Ministry of Labour, Papers on Migration and Mobility in Northern England*, No. 6, Department of Geography, University of Newcastle, January.

Labour, Ministry of (1961), 'Distribution of Earnings of Manual Workers in October 1960', *Ministry of Labour Gazette*, April and June.

Labour, Ministry of (1966), 'Characteristics of the Wholly Unemployed', *Ministry of Labour Gazette*, April and July.

Lambert, Royston (1964), *Nutrition in Britain, 1950–1960*, Occasional Papers on Social Administration, No. 6, Codicote Press, Welwyn.

Land, Hilary (1966), *Large Families in London*, Occasional Papers in Social Administration, Bell.

Lewis, Oscar (1966), *La Vida*, Random House.

Little, Alan (1966), 'Low-Wage Earners' in OECD, *Low-Income Groups and Methods of Dealing with their Problems*, Papers for a Trade Union Seminar, Supplement to the Report, Paris, OECD.

Lydall, Harold (1968), *The Structure of Earnings*, Oxford University Press.

Lynes, Tony (1963), *National Assistance and National Prosperity*, Occasional Papers on Social Administration, No. 5, Codicote Press, Welwyn.

Marquand, Judith (1967), 'Which are the Lower-Paid Workers?', *British Journal of Industrial Relations*, November, pp. 359–74.

Marris, Peter (1958), *Widows and their Families*, Routledge.

Marris, Peter and Rein, Martin (1967), *Dilemmas of Social Reform*, Routledge and Kegan Paul.

Marsden, Dennis (1969), *Mothers Alone: Poverty and the Fatherless Family*, Penguin, revised paperback edition, 1973. (Summary in Townsend, 1970, pp. 205–219.)

Miller, S. M. (1966), 'Poverty', *World Congress of Sociology 1966*, Evian.

Morris, Pauline (1969), *Put Away*, Routledge.

National Assistance Board (1969), *Homeless Single Persons*, HMSO.

National Board for Prices and Incomes (1971), *General Problems of Low Pay*, Cmnd. 4684, HMSO.

139

National Committee on Commonwealth Immigrants (1967), *Areas of Special Housing Need*.

Pahl, R. A. (1971), 'Poverty and the Urban System', in *Spatial Problems of the British Economy*, edited by Chisholm, M. D. and Manners, G., Cambridge University Press.

Parkin, Frank (1971), *Class Inequality and Political Order: Social Stratification in Capitalist and Communist Societies*, MacGibbon & Kee.

Pensions and National Insurance, Ministry of (1966), *Financial and Other Circumstances of Retirement Pensioners*, HMSO.

Rex, John and Moore, Robert (1967), *Race, Community and Conflict*, Oxford University Press.

Robinson, Derek (1967), 'Low-Paid Workers and Incomes Policy', *Bulletin of the Oxford University Institute of Economics and Statistics*, February, pp. 1–29.

Routh, Guy (1965), *Occupation and Pay in Great Britain, 1906–60*, Cambridge University Press, for N.I.E.S.R.

Rowntree, B. Seebohm (1901), *Poverty: A Study of Town Life*, Macmillan.

Rowntree, B. Seebohm (1941), *Poverty and Progress*, Longmans.

Rowntree, B. Seebohm and Lavers, G. R. (1951), *Poverty and the Welfare State*, Longmans.

Runciman, W. G. (1966), *Relative Deprivation and Social Justice*, Routledge.

Sainsbury, Sally (1971), *Registered as Disabled*.

Seebohm Report (1968), *Report of the Committee on Local Authority and Allied Personal Services*, Cmnd. 3703, HMSO.

Shanas, E., Townsend, P., Wedderburn, D., Friis, H., Milhoj, P. and Stehouwer, J. (1968), *The Old in Three Industrial Societies* (Denmark, Britain, U.S.A.), Routledge.

Shaw, L. (1958), 'Living on a State-maintained Income, I', *Case Conference*, Vol. 4, No. 9, March.

Sinfield, Adrian (1967a), *Unemployed in Shields* (draft) University of Essex, (summary in Townsend, 1970).

Sinfield, Adrian (1967b), 'Poverty Research in Britain and Europe', *Conference on Poverty Research*, Bureau of Social Science Research, Washington. (An updated and substantially revised paper is to appear in Lipset, S. M. and Miller, S. M. (eds), *Poverty and Inequality*, Basic Books.)

Sinfield, Adrian and Twine, Fred (1969), 'The Working Poor', *Poverty*, Child Poverty Action Group, No. 12–13.

Social Science Research Council (1968), *Research on Poverty*, Heinemann.

Social Security, Ministry of (1967), *Circumstances of Families*, HMSO.

Tawney, R. H. (1964), *Equality*, with a new introduction by Richard M. Titmuss, Allen & Unwin.

Thompson, E. P. and Yeo, Eileen (1971), *The Unknown Mayhew*, Merlin Press.

Titmuss, Richard (1958), *Essays on the Welfare State*, Allen & Unwin.

Titmuss, Richard (1962), *Income Distribution and Social Change*, Allen & Unwin.

Titmuss, Richard (1965), 'Poverty vs. Inequality: Diagnosis', *The Nation*, No. 200, 8 February, pp. 130–3.

Townsend, Peter (1962a), 'The Meaning of Poverty', *British Journal of Sociology*, September, pp. 210–27.

Townsend, Peter (1962b), *The Last Refuge: A Survey of Residential Institutions and Homes for the Aged in England and Wales*, Routledge.

Townsend, Peter (1963), *The Family Life of Old People*, Routledge. (Revised with new concluding chapter, Penguin, 1963.)

Townsend, Peter (1967a), *Poverty, Socialism and Labour in Power*, Fabian Tract No. 371. (Also in *Socialism and Affluence: Four Fabian Essays* (by Brian Abel-Smith, Richard Titmuss, Richard Crossman and Peter Townsend) Fabian Society, 1967.)

Townsend, Peter (1967b), *The Disabled in Society*, Greater London Association for the Disabled.

Townsend, Peter (1967c), 'Measures and Explanations of Poverty in High Income and Low Income Countries: The Problems of Operationalising the Concepts of Development', *International Seminar on Poverty*, University of Essex (published in Townsend 1970).

Townsend, Peter (ed.) (1970), *The Concept of Poverty: Working Papers on Methods of Investigation and Life-Styles of the Poor in Different Countries*, Heinemann.

Townsend, Peter (1973), *Poverty in the United Kingdom*, (First report of the LSE/University of Essex Survey into Inequality and the Distribution of Resources), Allen & Unwin.

Townsend, Peter and Bosanquet, Nicholas (1972), *Labour and Inequality*, Fabian Society.

Townsend, Peter and Wedderburn, Dorothy (1965), *The Aged in the Welfare State: The Interim Report of a Survey of Persons Aged 65 and Over in Britain, 1962 and 1963*, Occasional Papers on Social Administration, No. 14, Bell.

Tunstall, Jeremy (1966), *Old and Alone*, Routledge.

United Nations (1967), *Incomes in Post-War Europe: A Study of Policies, Growth and Distribution* (Economic Survey of Europe in 1965: Part 2) Economic Commission for Europe.

Veit-Wilson, John (1967), *The Resources of the Disabled*, (draft), University of Essex.

Wedderburn, Dorothy (1965), *Redundancy and the Railwaymen*, University of Cambridge, Department of Applied Economics, Occasional Papers No. 4, Cambridge University Press.

Wedderburn, Dorothy (1970), 'Inequality in the Workplace', *New Society*, 9th April.

Willmott, Phyllis and Peter (1963), 'Off Work Through Illness', *New Society*, 10th January, pp. 16–18.

Wilson, Harriet (1962), *Delinquency and Child Neglect*, Allen & Unwin.

Wynn, M. (1970), *Family Policy*, Michael Joseph.

Chapter 8

Half-way to a Motorized Society

J. MICHAEL THOMSON

The British nation has gone about half-way towards the creation of a motorized society, in the sense that the number of cars has now reached about half the forecast saturation level of 45 cars per hundred people, i.e. just over two people per car. It has taken seventy years to come this far, but the remaining distance could be largely covered in another twenty years and will almost certainly be so in thirty years. We can confidently predict that by the end of the century almost every household that wants a car will have one. No government is likely to do anything that substantially alters this fact. The growth of two-car households, on the other hand, is much more susceptible to influence and hence less certain; looking further ahead, therefore, we may have to change our assessment of the saturation level. But the important fact is that universal family car ownership is now within the sights of present-day planning. New roads, railways, airports, shopping centres, new towns and other major building developments can and must be planned on the assumption of general car ownership. We are no longer just speculating about the motorized society, we are actually designing it.

This means that we have entered a period of history—probably quite a short period—in which we have to make and are already making decisions that will vitally affect the future way of life in this country for a long time. The decisions we make now, concerning the accommodation of the car, are going to determine the *kind* of motorized society that eventually takes shape. Fortunately, being in this position so much later than the Americans, we can learn from their experience.

The original American concept of a motorized society was based on the presumption that the car was inherently superior to all other forms of ground transport for all journeys. The ideal motorized society was, therefore, one in which all land journeys could be made comfortably, speedily and safely by car. The efforts to create this sort of society have, however, caused enormous problems and sacrifices and have produced a current wave of 'anti-auto, anti-highway sentiment', especially among the younger generation.

142

One does not have to be anti-car or anti-highway to realize that this extreme concept of the *fully motorized society* is not always attainable or worth the sacrifices involved. An alternative concept is a *selectively motorized society*, in which cars are generally available and are used when they offer clear advantages but are not always used for all purposes. This concept denies the inherent superiority of the car; it does not assume that a car must always be preferred to public transport. It accepts that facilities for public and private transport can and should be provided in such a way that car-owners, weighing up cost, speed, parking problems, comfort, reliability and so on, will sometimes prefer to use public transport.

In short, the aim of this concept of a selectively motorized society is to secure the *main* advantages of the private car for everybody without incurring its worst disadvantages. A compromise has to be struck between the full use of the car and its unfortunate side effects. The extent and nature of this compromise will vary greatly between town and country, between different towns and between different parts of a town. Before discussing this, however, let us establish just what are the main advantages and disadvantages of the car.

ADVANTAGES OF THE CAR

It is important for policy-makers to distinguish between the *inherent* advantages of the car and those advantages which are, or may be, *determined* by policy. The three main inherent advantages are:

Instant Availability

All forms of public transport require a certain amount of walking and waiting. (Under current development, however, are the dial-a-bus, which eliminates the walk to the bus stop, and the high speed travelator and auto-taxi, both of which eliminate waiting.) The relative advantage of not having to walk or wait is much greater on short journeys than on long ones. Commonly, a five-minute journey by car is a 20-minute journey by public transport, simply on account of the walking and waiting time. It is not possible on short journeys, as it may be on long ones, for public transport to offset this disadvantage in other ways.

Door-to-door Transport of 'Awkward' Loads

This obviously includes heavy parcels, shopping baskets and suitcases but it also includes awkward human loads, such as small children, very old people, invalids and so on. In most of these cases it is the minimization of effort and inconvenience, rather than journey time, that is important. Most of these journeys are very short—to the shops, nursery school, doctor, station, etc.

The Ability to make Some Journeys Conveniently which cannot be made Conveniently, if at all, by Public Transport

On a fully-developed public transport system (which of course may not exist) it is, by definition, *possible* to travel between any two points, given a certain amount of walking, but there is no way of designing the system so that all journeys are equally convenient. The necessity to change vehicle, once or more than once, on many journeys is inevitable, whereas with the car this is inherently unnecessary. This advantage can occur on both long and short journeys but it tends to be more significant when it occurs on short journeys.

In terms of the numbers of journeys affected these three advantages seem to be much the most important advantages inherent in the technology of the car. Then there are others which, though not inherent, often arise in practice, as follows:

Vehicle Speed

Cars are often faster than public transport, but technologically both trains and cars could travel much faster than they usually do in practice. Bus services could also be operated faster if given traffic priority. The relative speeds of public and private transport, therefore, depend not on inherent technological limitations but on investment and management policies.

Cost

The use of the car is quite often cheaper, or seems cheaper, than public transport. In many instances, however, the true (marginal) costs—social and economic—of using the car are higher, both to the user and much more so to the community, than the user appreciates. Public transport fares, on the other hand, are often much higher than the marginal costs of using such transport. In both cases the price to the user can be significantly altered by government policy, especially through taxes and subsidies.

Comfort

The comfort of car travel depends significantly on the provision of straight, free-flowing roads, i.e. on government investment. The comfort of public transport depends even more on investment, in

144

good rolling stock and in capacity to avoid overcrowding. So, again, the relative attraction of public and private transport can be swayed by policy decisions.

In all these matters, the longer the journey the easier it is to increase the relative attractiveness of public transport; and we have already seen that the inherent advantages of the car tend to lie in short journeys. The implication is clear. If it is necessary, as sometimes it is, to plan for a situation in which car-owners will continue to make some journeys by public transport, let these be in general the longer journeys.

DISADVANTAGES OF THE CAR

The problems caused by the car can be grouped under seven headings:

Provision of Roads

The two main aspects are cost and displacement. Motorways are the cheapest way of accommodating large volumes of traffic; their cost varies from less than £1 million a mile in rural areas to £20 millions a mile in, for example, Inner London. The extremely high cost in heavily built-up areas is due not just to the high cost of land but also to the construction problems posed by existing roads, railways, underground services and other obstacles.

The question of displacement is not so difficult in rural areas, where housing and important buildings can usually be circumvented, but is unavoidable in urban areas. The extreme example is again Inner London, where motorways would directly displace about 1,000 persons per mile. House-owners would naturally receive a fair market price for their property but most of them would feel resentful, since they do not wish to sell at the market price. If, however, it were possible to pay them 50 per cent above the market price most of them would probably be glad to sell, and this problem would be overcome.

Although motorways can carry much larger traffic volumes than other roads and are consequently the cheapest way of providing new road capacity, not all new capacity can be provided in this form. Motorways are the broad channels into which large numbers of vehicles with different origins and destinations must be fed via a finer network of main distributor roads and a still finer network of local distributor roads. In rural areas and small towns, when motorways are built, the existing roads normally have sufficient capacity to feed the motorways and serve local traffic; the shortage of road capacity can then be overcome simply by building the motorways or other high-capacity new roads.

In large cities, however, because of the high density of (potential) medium distance traffic—i.e. neither local nor long distance, but intra-city traffic using the motorways—the existing roads can easily prove inadequate to serve as distributors to a motorway system, depending on numerous factors including the size of and access frequency to the motorways. Hence, if one introduces motorways into large cities one may need to widen many other roads in order to enable the motorways to operate efficiently at their designed capacity. This is liable to add considerably to the amount and cost of property displacement.

Provision of Parking Space

As the number of cars visiting a given centre increases, the average cost of parking is almost certain to increase, in either economic or social terms. The *economic* cost of parking can be held down only by increasing the area of ground-level parking—on or off the street— at the expense of traffic movement, environment and, eventually, other activities. These *social* costs of parking can be contained only by providing multi-storey or underground car parks, which, of course, are costly in economic terms.

Impact on the Environment

Concern about the environment has now become fashionable, and doubtless it is not just a passing fancy. There is no need to catalogue here the ways in which traffic and highways can damage the environment. But it is worth noting that a number of different attitudes towards the problem are emerging. The days may be gone when one could dismiss environmentalists as sentimental enemies of progress, or when one could conveniently assume that people would get used to anything. But this does not mean that everyone is now agreed, even in principle, on how to treat the environmental question. Five distinct approaches are discernible: the 'engineering' approach that everything 'within reason' should be done to minimize the adverse effects of a project—say, a motorway—on the environment, but 'within reason' never includes the possible rejection of the project itself on environmental grounds; the 'amenity' approach that the project should not be accepted if it cannot be designed in a way that does not lower the quality of the environment: this attitude does not necessarily rule out the building of motorways but it can certainly add greatly to their cost and in some places make them completely unacceptable; the 'planning' approach that environmental standards should be laid down and observed: the danger here, as with all standards, is that they will set a minimum level which will be adhered to both in places where it is unjustifiably costly and in places where a higher standard could be justified; the 'economic' approach that methods should be developed for calculating values for environmental factors so that they could be weighed together with the other costs and benefits of a motorway project: even if these values have to be determined crudely and subjectively they are still, so it is argued, the best available way of handling the environmental question; lastly, the 'judicial' approach that the problem would cease to be a problem if those adversely affected could be fully compensated: according to this view the solution lies in more liberal and sophisticated compensation.

The labelling of these different ways of looking at the question is not intended to suggest that the different professions are in sharp conflict but simply that they tend to view the environmental problem in rather different ways.

Impact on Non-Motorists

Possibly the greatest weakness in the concept of a motorized society is the fact that a large proportion of the population will remain without cars, either because they are not able or permitted to drive or because the household car is being used by someone else or is otherwise not available. For this reason alone a fully motorized society is not a practical possibility in a socially-conscious country. There must remain a public transport system. Without public transport the possession of only one car in the household becomes synonymous with poverty. Even if motorists gain a genuine advantage in 'mobility' under such a system—and we shall discuss the question of mobility presently—this extra mobility may not be justifiable if it can be achieved only by a severe loss of mobility for non-motorists. The vital questions, therefore, arise: What kind of public transport service is going to be maintained in the face of dwindling demand and how is it going to be financed? An inescapable fact about public transport is that, except when it is operating above designed capacity, a decline in the volume of passengers tends to cause either an increase in the average cost per passenger-mile or a reduction in the quality of service—primarily by cuts in service frequency—or both. Higher fares and lower quality of service both lead to further losses of passengers. The burden of paying rising fares for a worsening service falls mainly on the young, the old, the poor and the disabled.

It is possible in principle, and it may become necessary in practice, to determine as a matter of public policy that a certain quality of public transport service *must* be provided, i.e. that certain services *must* be maintained at specified levels of frequency and comfort, regardless of commercial viability. Such a policy would help to safeguard the interest of non-motorists. It would also highlight the fact that when a person decides to leave public transport in favour of a car he leaves a cost—in both real and money terms—for someone else to bear. Seen in this light, it may be argued that motorists should not be permitted to pursue their own advantage *at other people's expense*, and that a logical and equitable case therefore exists for subsidizing public transport out of motor taxation. This is now being done in West Germany.

Other ways in which the non-motorist is affected by a motorized society are discussed below in the context of land use and social effects.

Accidents

All forms of transport are dangerous. Purely from a safety point of view there is an advantage in ordering our activities so that we make fewer and shorter journeys by any given method. Of the different modes available most people would agree that private motor vehicles are the most subject to accidents. Road casualties in this country are currently numbering about 7,000 deaths and 90,000 serious injuries each year. Although these figures have not grown anything like as fast as the volume of traffic, thanks to innumerable safety improvements, there can be little doubt that the figures will grow higher as traffic increases over the next twenty years, and that measures which have the effect of slowing down the growth of traffic are likely to reduce the number of transport accidents as a whole.

The toll of traffic accidents is equivalent to a large number of major catastrophes every year. Most people appear willing to accept this as part of the price of motorization. To the individual there is a statistical *risk*, which he usually ignores, that in the next year he may be killed or seriously injured on the roads. But to the community it is a statistical *certainty*, which should not be ignored, that in the next year approximately 100,000 of its members will meet such a fate. This is an important part of the price of motorization, and should be taken into account whenever policies concerning it are in question.

Effects on Land Use

We now come to two important, interesting, but little understood, aspects of motorization. Although we discuss them under the heading 'disadvantages of the car' they may well have advantages too. The first aspect is the effect of motorization on land use. Our land area and its main natural features are virtually fixed; and nearly all of it is used for some purpose, either productive or amenity or both. The way in which the land is divided between different uses (or, conversely, activities are located over the land) is of fundamental importance and is determined by numerous factors of which the availability, speed and cost of transport are highly influential.

A crucial difference between the car and all forms of public transport is that, whereas the public transport user naturally prefers his activities to be located along corridors well served by public transport, the car user is not so constrained. Both the motorist and the non-motorist are much concerned with door-to-door journey speed but, while the public transport user is likely to improve his journey speed if he goes with the crowd, the motorist is likely to do better if he avoids the crowd (especially when he wants to park). Hence, it is in the interest of public transport users to concentrate their activities, while motorists are strongly drawn to a more dispersed pattern of activities.

This is indeed a crucial matter, especially for an old-established community that has developed largely on the pattern set long ago by an elaborate railway system fed by slow-moving, horse-drawn vehicles, both public and private. The basic *form* of our cities, towns and even villages is unsuited to the general use of cars. Some people might argue that cars are an unsuitable means of transport for general use in large cities of *any* form, but certainly this is true of the traditional, centralized form of city. No one has found a way of designing or redesigning a city centre, with its traditional functions, so as to permit full motorization.

It might be possible to transform the structure of our communities by wholesale dispersal policies, so as to conform to the 'natural' requirements of motorization, although this would be extremely difficult in large cities. But what is not possible is to restructure a city in a form suitable for motorization and, at the same time, to retain a form suitable for public transport. The more dispersed the big traffic-generating activities become, the more difficult (i.e. the more costly) it becomes for public transport to serve those activities.

The prime forces towards dispersal are the demand for parking space, the cost of land and uncongested road access. Shops, hotels,

149

pubs, restaurants and clubs are among the first activities to seek locations that are attractive to motorists, i.e. that are easy to drive to and have plenty of free parking space. As the level of car ownership rises, offices, research establishments and eventually even factories also seek locations where they can attract car-using labour. All these activities tend to become less accessible, sometimes quite inaccessible, to non-motorists, who thus find that public transport is not only declining and growing more expensive but also becoming less well-suited to their travel needs.

Planning controls may be able to guide and influence changes in land use of this kind. But, so far, we have been considering only changes in *what* the land is used for. Equally important are changes in *who* the land is used by, because both the volume and pattern of travel are highly dependent on how individuals choose to locate their various activities in relation to each other. The most important choice is the relative location of home and job. The peak-hour traffic problem is a result of many thousands or even millions of individual decisions on where to live and work. In any British city it is theoretically easy to reshuffle people among the *existing* homes, or jobs, or both, so as to double the volume of travel to work (i.e. the number of person-miles) and also to render the public transport system virtually useless. This kind of dispersal requires no changes in land *use*, merely changes in land *user*, over which there is no planning control. It is a natural consequence of reliance on the car, which tends gradually to lead to longer journeys not only for work but for other purposes, too, and to journeys being made in all directions, in a random fashion, and hence unsuitable for any known form of public transport.

These land-use effects partly explain why, in large urban areas, new roads tend to stimulate the growth of traffic and why, after the process of road-building and motorization has gone as far as it has in most American cities and there is still widespread congestion, there is little choice but to build more roads for yet more traffic because the land-use basis of a public transport system has largely vanished.

Social Implications

For many people the immediate, direct result of acquiring a car is that they simply switch from public transport to the car but go on making much the same journeys as before: the car is initially a convenience without any important social side effects. But the long-term effects of a lot of people acquiring cars can be of real social significance in many ways which have not been adequately investigated. The social impact arises not directly from the fact that some journeys are made faster and more conveniently than before, but indirectly from the consequential changes in the locational pattern of activities, in public transport and in the environment.

The most obvious social effect of the changing pattern of activities occurs in rural areas, because the frequency and availability of public transport in such areas cannot normally equal that in urban localities. Consequently, the possession of a car soon induces rural households to make numerous trips which they would not otherwise have made. Their style of life may thus be changed. More radical, however, is the effect of car ownership in inducing people to move out of urban areas to live in the country. Their style of life is obviously changed. If too many people do this, of course, the rural area ceases to be rural and the advantages sought by the first migrants into the area are diminished.

Nevertheless, whether or not the process goes too far, the effect of motorization is undoubtedly for many erstwhile city dwellers to establish themselves at relatively low density in relatively green areas. Whole communities are created on the basis of car ownership. The social implications are numerous and, on balance, are probably favourable.

In short, the car can transform life in rural areas and thus attract people to live there. Initially, these migrants from the city tend to commute to work in the city but, as the supply of labour in the rural (or by then semi-rural) areas increases, there is a tendency for employment to move out to those areas also.

At the same time, however, the uncontrolled impact of this process on both the location of activities and the effectiveness of public transport leads directly to the creation of a new underprivileged class: the transport poor, those without access to a car. This problem occurs in both urban and rural areas but is more obvious in the latter. It is not simply that people without cars in rural areas are stranded if the local bus service is withdrawn or reduced below a minimal frequency; they may also be unable to get to activities located far from a bus route, and these activities increasingly embrace not only public places frequented by motorists but also the homes of car-owning households themselves. Hence, there are powerful forces tending to divide those who have cars from those who do not. The same process occurs in cities, though less dramatically; people are not so easily stranded in cities but they may in practice become less and less mobile in the sense of not being able to go where they want without increasing discomfort, delay and expense.

MOBILITY

This brings us to the question of *mobility*. Transport plans are often put forward with the aim of increasing mobility, which is taken to be a meaningful and desirable thing. But what is mobility? According to one definition it is the freedom to travel where and when one wishes. If one accepts that 'freedom' means an absence of constraints, such as delay, discomfort, cost, uncertainty and danger, then one must consider whether it is always desirable to increase this freedom. Completely unconstrained movement (infinite mobility) would bring enormous problems of staggering dimensions. There is obviously no question of removing all the constraints on movement. Nevertheless, the trend towards greater freedom of movement has already produced considerable problems of environment, congested facilities and cost in places as diverse as the Lake District, the French Riviera and Central London.

More relevant to the present discussion, however, is the second part of the definition of mobility: 'to travel where and when one wishes'. This poses the questions: Where and when do people really wish to travel? Clearly, it depends on where and when various activities take place and on people wanting to go to them. An improvement in mobility is not just a matter of being able to travel more freely; it is also a question of wanting to go to activities that occur in places and at times that are accessible. The man who travels ten miles at 10 m.p.h. is not obviously less mobile than the man who travels twenty miles at twenty m.p.h. to reach the same place. The man who moves out of the city to obtain easier use of his car is not necessarily more mobile if some of the city activities which he values highly thereby become inaccessible to him.

When people buy their first car they are generally seeking to improve their mobility. How far they can achieve collectively what they are all quite sensibly seeking individually depends on how much road and parking space is provided, how far public transport is allowed to decline (because car-owners still wish to use public transport sometimes), how widely dispersed their activities and social contacts become, and by how much the direct cost of transport—in taxes, fares, parking fees, etc—rises in the process. Only after assessing the way in which all these factors have changed as a result of motorization can one judge how far car-owners have actually succeeded in increasing their mobility. In rural areas and doubtless in many small towns, car-owners have genuinely achieved a much higher level of mobility. In some cities, notably ones without rail networks, where the growth of car ownership has choked traffic movement, saturated the parking space, ruined the bus services, jeopardized movement by foot or bicycle and undermined the prosperity of the city centre, it is possible—though difficult to prove—that car-owners are no more mobile than they would have been if none of them had acquired cars (or at least if they had decided not to use their cars for journeys within the city). But whether this is so or not, there is little question that in many cities, as the number of car-owners increases, the mobility of existing car-owners declines. So too, of course, does that of those without cars. The incentive to own a car may therefore actually increase, in spite of the declining mobility it provides.

This is why one should be a little careful in referring to the gains in mobility afforded by the car. Certainly, at any point in time the car-owner will appear to be considerably more mobile than the non-car-owner, but, in the long run, it is not so obvious how much extra mobility the whole process of motorization brings to car-owners in large cities. Whatever these gains may be, they have to be set against any loss of mobility by non-car-owners and possibly, in extreme cases, against the implications of dividing society sharply between 'transport haves' and 'transport have nots'.

The big difficulty with the 'have nots' is that, although there are so many of them, even in a fully motorized society, they are unable on their own to support a satisfactory public transport system through the payment of fares. There are three main reasons for this. The 'have nots' possess little purchasing power, because they consist largely of old age pensioners, children, invalids and low-income households; they are sensitive to the level of fares. Because of the sort of people they are, their travel requirements are relatively small, though nonetheless important to them. In a highly motorized society wage levels will be high, and public transport, being labour-intensive, will be correspondingly costly to operate.

The transport poor fall naturally into members of non-car-owning households and car-less members of car-owning households. The former households include many retired old people who, deprived of adequate transport, may simply opt for a quiet life. Younger households without a car may be obliged to migrate—from the country to the towns and from the suburbs towards the city centres where public transport is usually better. In households with only one car, if the wage earner finds it necessary to drive to work the rest of the family is car-less for much of the time.

MAKING THE DECISIONS

We come back to the fact that this country is now in the position of having to decide, not as a nation but town by town, county by county, what kind of a motorized society it is going to try to create. The potential advantages of motorization are simple, but immense; the potential disadvantages are also immense, but not so simple. The magnitudes of the advantages and disadvantages vary greatly from place to place, and especially between city, town and country. Nothing would be worse than to produce a standardized solution for general application. In particular, London is a special case, not comparable even with the other conurbations, on account of its exceptional size and dependence on rail transport.

How then are the decisions to be made? What roads and what kinds of roads should be built? How is the traffic going to be limited to that whose social and economic costs are worth meeting? What public transport system needs to be provided? What steps must be taken to safeguard pedestrian interests and to protect and improve the environment? What controls are to be applied to land use? How is the whole system to be financed and managed through taxes, fares, subsidies?

The same basic questions have to be asked everywhere but the answers will be very different. In the past many bad decisions have been made. There is little hope of getting better decisions in future unless two basic conditions are met. First, the institutional machinery must enable long-term strategic planning to be carried out comprehensively, i.e. covering all forms of transport and related matters over a large enough area. Recent governments have made big efforts to reorganize local government and transport authorities in order to make this comprehensive approach possible, especially in the conurbations. We are undoubtedly better organized than ever before—and than most other countries—to make good decisions.

Secondly, there must be a rational *method* of arriving at decisions. Until recently strategic planning decisions, and road-building decisions in particular, where made either on highly deficient reasoning or on plain intuition. An enormous amount of research has been undertaken in the last ten or fifteen years to uncover the facts about travel behaviour and traffic performance, to determine the cost relationships and to develop techniques for predicting and evaluating the effects of alternative planning strategies. Inevitably, *cost-benefit analysis* has been taken up as the only way of introducing objectivity into the making of these difficult decisions.

It is to the credit of government departments that they have done so much to encourage and develop the cost-benefit approach because without it there is little hope of rescuing planning from the arena of power politics.

Given present institutions and the growing adoption of a cost-benefit approach, this country is quite well placed to make some sensible decisions about the problems of motorization. Let us look briefly at the kind of solutions that may be adopted.

TRUNK ROADS

The least difficult of our traffic problems, and the one that has been tackled first, is that of inter-city traffic. There is no technical or economic reason why the greater part of inter-city traffic should not eventually be accommodated on fast, relatively safe motorways or dual-carriageway all-purpose roads. Holiday and summer weekend peak traffic may, however, present an insoluble problem, since new road capacity may never be worth providing in order to eliminate delays that occur only a few times each year.

There is practically no opposition to the national motorway programme as a whole, although there is inevitably local opposition to every choice of alignment. The roads lobby claims, of course that we are doing too little too late and are lagging years behind other countries. The cost-benefit analysis of the M1 between London and Birmingham suggested, however, that that motorway was built at just the right time; the investment would not have been justified any sooner.

Cost-benefit analysis was applied to the trunk road programme long before urban roads because the practical problems were less formidable. The technical information and predictive techniques developed over the last ten years by the Ministry of Transport are probably good enough now to give a very fair idea of the right priorities and timing to be given to the trunk road programme. It is not difficult to obtain a good cost-benefit return on inter-city road projects, looking to the growth of traffic over the next thirty years, but the proper timing of such projects requires that a satisfactory return should be achieved from the first normal year of operation. It may well be that some foreign countries have invested too rapidly in motorways and that this country has in fact been right to hold back on them in order to accelerate its programmes for houses, schools and hospitals.

THE RURAL PROBLEM

There is no difficulty in accommodating the local use of the car in rural areas by modest improvements to existing roads. The rural problem concerns non-motorists and the bus services on which they depend. The last government accepted the case for subsidizing rural bus services, provided that the local county authorities would contribute an equal share. Not many counties have been willing to participate to any great extent and, as a result, bus services continue to dwindle. The amount of money needed to keep rural bus services solvent is, in fact, quite tiny in comparison with other public expenditure on transport.

There is no solution to the rural problem other than the provision of bus subsidies. The only question is who is going to provide them. If they are not provided many poorer people will drift into the towns and those who cannot do so, especially the very young and very old, will suffer a lower quality of life. The problem is certainly not intractable, because the amount of money involved is so modest. It would be unfortunate if the problem remained unsolved, because of meanness or dogmatic belief in the profit test.

SMALL TOWNS

Coming to the urban problem, it is necessary to distinguish between different sizes of town. In small towns the problem can be seen as one mainly of design. Most small towns suffer from a high proportion of through traffic until a by-pass is built. The next task is to redesign the local traffic circulation in the town centre, so that traffic can move around and park close to the centre point—usually a single square or intersection—without crossing it.

With careful design and moderate expenditure, full motorization can usually be achieved in small towns of up to 50,000—70,000 population, without serious environmental or social impact. Land-use implications are likely to be minimal in such small areas. Local bus services are usually the last stages of rural bus services, but in towns of this size most internal journeys are within walking or cycling distance.

LARGE TOWNS AND CITIES

In towns of up to about 250,000 population it is probably possible, both physically and financially, to cater for full motorization, i.e. for maximum use of cars; but this may not be desirable. In larger towns and cities it is not in practice possible; the question of desirability therefore does not arise. In all large towns and cities it is, therefore, necessary to consider alternative conceptions of motorization which do not allow for unlimited use of cars.

An essential point which soon emerges from any study of urban transport planning is that the difficulties of providing roads and parking space for motor traffic tend to increase sharply as one approaches the city centre from the periphery. Construction becomes more difficult, land and property values rise steeply, the unavoidable displacement of high-density housing becomes a major problem, the environmental damage is more difficult to deal with and affects more people,'the impact on public transport tends to be greater. Many cities recognize that the cost and damage of bringing new roads into the city centre itself cannot be justified, even though it is in the city centre that the lack of road space appears to be greatest. In other words, as one approaches the centre, the costs—social and economic —of new roads rise faster than do the benefits and there is a limit inside which new roads are in general not worth-while. The disadvantages exceed the benefits. It is the *distance in* from the edge of the city rather than the *distance out* from the centre that seems to determine the limit. This is important, because it suggests that the larger city the larger the area round the centre in which new roads are likely to be ruled out on cost-benefit grounds.

Clearly, this conclusion is highly generalized and may be subject to many exceptions. But the point holds true that there is no justification for assuming that the same kind of road network or transport system is right for cities of very different sizes.

We may conclude, then, that, whereas in small towns full use of the car may be planned for, in larger towns and cities there will be an area in the centre where only limited use of the car is worth planning for, and this area will tend to be larger in the larger cities. This area may for practical purposes be divided into an outer band in which the use of the car need be limited only during the peak hours, i.e. mainly for journeys to and from work, and a central area in which the use of the car for other purposes needs also to be limited. Only in the largest cities is the latter degree of limitation likely to be required. These cities will then consist of a central area where the use of cars is severely limited, an inner area where it is limited for work journeys, and an outer area where it is not limited except possibly in some big suburban employment centres during peak hours. In other, smaller cities there would be only the latter two areas.

WAYS OF LIMITING THE USE OF CARS IN CITIES

One must distinguish between methods of traffic *restraint* and methods of traffic *avoidance*. Restraint occurs when motorists are dissuaded by parking controls, road pricing, congestion, or other deterrents, from fulfilling *conscious desires* to use their cars. They may respond to the restraint by using public transport instead, by not making the journey at all, or by making a different journey, e.g. at a different time, or a shorter journey by car or by some other method, or a journey partly by car and partly by public transport.

One of the outstanding needs at the present time is to develop more sophisticated methods of traffic restraint. Currently, we have to rely on haphazard and inefficient parking controls and on the fortuitous effects of congestion. Parking controls are not yet well related to the capacity of the road system (for which they are a rationing device) and they are avoided by a large number of motorists who have access to uncontrolled parking space. Congestion is, and is likely to remain, an important instrument for keeping down the volume of traffic but so far no attempt has been made to plan congestion like crowd control, i.e. to plan where the queues should form. Traffic methods, originally designed to increase the traffic capacity of road networks, are now beginning to be used for other purposes, such as the protection of the environment and the implementation of bus priorities. They can be used also for traffic restraint.

The most important development in traffic restraint, however, is likely to be road pricing, that is, the charging of direct prices—rather than indirect taxes—for using valuable road space. Road pricing gets at the root of the problem of traffic congestion by charging motorists an appropriate price for the use of assets that are in great demand and exceedingly costly to expand. Many systems of road pricing have been canvassed over the last ten years and three systems have been selected for advanced development by the Road Research Laboratory. Depending on the system adopted, a car (or any other vehicle to which the system were applied) would carry either a meter or an electronically-identifiable plate. The meter would be controlled by means of electric circuits in the road and would be either prepaid or periodically inspected and billed for, like an electricity meter. The identity plate would serve to pass information to a computer which would eventually produce a bill, as with the telephone system. Either way, the motorist would be charged every time he passed over a pricing point, and the density of active pricing points would vary according to the area and time of day or week. Hence, a highly sophisticated means of traffic restraint would be available which could replace a large part of existing motor taxation as a revenue earner and replace parking controls as the principal regulator of traffic demand.

Traffic restraint plays the role normally played by prices in limiting demand. *Traffic avoidance* aims to influence the factors that generate demand in the first place. Most industries have little influence (other than through marketing methods) over the factors that determine demand for their products. Planning authorities, by contrast, have many ways of influencing people's travel desires. The location of land use, inasmuch as it can be controlled by planning powers, can influence the average length of journeys and also the choice of mode. The improvement of public transport can reduce the demand for private transport. The provision of medium-speed roads instead of high-speed motorways can reduce journey lengths and favour the use of fast rail transport. The provision of convenient car parks at stations—with prices below those at car parks nearer the city centre —can tempt motorists to park and ride. Priorities can improve the competitive position of the buses, which suffer unfairly from the lack of pricing for scarce road space and parking space; the techniques for giving buses priority are still in an early stage of development.

In these and other ways people can be persuaded to *choose* patterns of activity and movement (and, most important, to keep to these patterns where they already exist) which involve fewer and shorter car journeys, especially for getting to work, and more journeys by foot, cycle, bus, train and possibly taxi. The aim of traffic avoidance is that people, while undertaking the same kind of social and economic activities, will not require to travel as often or as far by car within the city as they otherwise would.

LONDON

As already mentioned, London is a special case, on account of its enormous size and its traditional reliance on rail transport. The great issue in London, at present, is how far to bring what kind of roads into the city. In particular, is the Greater London Council wise to propose a network of four ring-motorways at distances approximately three, seven, twelve and eighteen miles from the centre?

The real issue here, which the current public inquiry is trying to settle, is not what is usually conveyed by the newspapers. It is not a question of houses and environment versus efficient transport. The real issue is whether the ringways—the two inner ones especially —will significantly improve London's transport efficiency. Will they in practice make any real difference to traffic congestion in Inner London or will they simply generate so much more traffic—through land-use effects, transfer from public transport, stimulation of two-car ownership and increasing journey lengths—that they will put as much traffic back on to the other roads as they draw off them? If this is so, then these inner motorways—however much they may *seem* to be needed—will do little good, except to a small proportion of long-distance traffic, and will undoubtedly do a great deal of harm to the environment and the housing situation at enormous cost in terms of money, impact on public transport and additional accidents.

159

Transport is full of paradoxes, and one of them is that the places where new roads seem to be most needed are often the places where they will do least good. This is clearly the case in Central London. The worst congestion in London can be found along Oxford Street and through the heart of the City, but no one is proposing road-building as the solution. The reason is simply that in areas of very high travel activity people can easily see that the private car is not suitable as the main means of travel, because of the space it requires and the noise and pollution it brings.

The basic problem in London is to determine over how wide an area of Inner London the need extends for solutions designed to limit the mileage that people will desire to clock up in their cars.

The alternative strategy for Inner London, if the inner motorways are abandoned, could be to cater for the short-distance use of cars, i.e. the innumerable local trips that people like to make by car, and also for car trips out of London, but to do everything possible to persuade people to use rail and underground for longer trips within London. This strategy might involve: small-town treatment for suburban centres in Inner London, i.e. by-pass arrangements for through-traffic, and town centre redevelopment to facilitate local circulation, parking and pedestrian movement; all-round improvements to the quality of public transport, especially service frequencies; much more convenient, cheap parking space at stations; creation of a continuous bus priority network, embracing main bus routes and employing numerous traffic management measures to limit the volume of other traffic to a level compatible with efficient bus operation; high parking charges graduated upwards towards the city centre, but with residents' parking privileges; low fares on public transport financed partly out of parking revenues; environmental management to force through traffic out of residential areas.

CONCLUSION

The advantages of the motor car are simple and obvious. The use of cars needs no encouragement; indeed, the whole manner in which the costs of motorization are paid for favours the use of cars. The disadvantages are more complex. This article suggests that the main advantages of the car can be enjoyed and the worst disadvantages avoided by policies designed to resist the undesirable trends inherent in motorized societies—notably those towards dispersal and the run-down of public transport—and by policies of traffic restraint and traffic avoidance in large towns and cities. These policies should be worked out not on doctrinaire grounds, but on objective analysis of the diverse costs and benefits likely to result.

We stand in this country half-way towards a motorized society. We have had time to learn from the mistakes of other countries. It would be sad and inexcusable if in thirty years' time we (or our children) should be seriously questioning, as are some people in America now, whether it was all worth while.

Chapter 9

Long-term Population Distribution in Great Britain—Review of the Study and Implications for Future Development

Report by an Inter-Departmental Study Group (HMSO, 1971)

This study has looked at a number of aspects of population growth and their likely future distribution within Great Britain and has considered some of the consequential planning implications. This chapter reviews the tentative conclusions that have emerged from the study and attempts to correlate them into a general framework.

POPULATION TRENDS AND FORECASTS

The study covers a span of two centuries, from the beginning of the last century to the end of this. In the 170 years from the first census of 1801 to 1970, the population of Great Britain has risen from 10·5 million to 54·2 million. The rate of future growth is clearly of vital importance in a country that is already one of the most densely populated in the world; currently, the population is forecast to rise by some 10 million by the end of the century. The reliability of population forecasting has been discussed and it is not without significance that the population projections to the end of the century have been revised downwards by nearly 9 million since the study was commissioned. But although too much reliance cannot be placed upon the precise size of the projected population at any given point in time, continuing growth currently seems the only reasonable basis for future planning.

CHANGES IN POPULATION DISTRIBUTION

The planning problems associated with continuing population growth stem more from the concentration of the population in a few relatively small areas than from its overall density. Viewed over the historical perspective of the study, the geographical pattern of population growth has been shifting, with the nineteenth century trend of higher than national growth rates in the North being reversed in the twentieth. The rapid urbanization of Britain in the

162

first half of the nineteenth century and associated rural depopulation has been followed this century by a marked outward expansion of the main urban areas. Today, with urban renewal, rising living and spatial standards, and greater mobility, there is a persistent movement of population from the inner areas of the towns and cities to their peripheries and beyond.

Changes in the distribution of population have in the past been largely a response to natural economic forces and improvements in transportation. From the 1930s onwards, successive Governments have sought directly or indirectly to influence population movements. Government action has been directed to maintaining employment opportunities and retaining population in the Development Areas; natural economic forces have worked in the opposite direction. The overall result has been that the geographical distribution of population has changed only gradually over time.

Since the war, the population of the South and Midlands as a whole has been growing faster than the North, Scotland and Wales notwithstanding policies to promote new employment in these areas. The differences have been largely due to migration between regions and more recently to migration to and from overseas. The economic forces which have been largely responsible for this trend of relatively faster population growth in the South and Midlands— particularly the decline in employment opportunities in mining, shipbuilding, textiles and other staple industries often heavily concentrated in the North, Scotland and Wales—seem likely to persist for some time yet. Economic and social considerations will consequently continue to give rise to pressures for the maintenance of positive policies to improve employment prospects in the problem areas.

Though the continuation of such policies could be expected over time to diminish net regional migration from the assisted areas, its future pattern is difficult to forecast, as the scale of gross migration tends to rise with a larger population, higher incomes and education, and as migration for environmental reasons (e.g. retirement) becomes more important. The rate of population growth will not therefore be uniform and some regions will continue to grow faster than others. Population forecasts are important initial inputs for the preparation of regional strategies, therefore tentative estimates of the population in 2001 have been made for each region, but in view of the uncertainties inherent in such projections, alternative figures are suggested in each case. Even so, strategies must have sufficient inbuilt flexibility to take account of changing circumstances, particularly of changing rates of population growth. The relationship of strategies to population growth is two-way, as the implementation of the strategies is intended to influence the rates of growth in the areas concerned.

FUTURE DEMAND FOR LAND

Having considered the likely future trends of population growth and distribution, the study considers the possible implications for the demand for land. The proportion of land in urban use has risen this century from 3·8 per cent of the total area in 1901 to 8·6 per cent in 1970. The growth of population, together with continuing urban redevelopment and rising spatial standards, will require a further substantial increase in urban land, possibly raising its proportion of the total to about 11 per cent by the end of the century. Much of the remainder is not of course available for urban use—there are major physical and policy constraints such as high land, national parks, areas of outstanding natural beauty and green belts. More than half of the land in the country comes into these categories which are, however, not of equal significance nor absolute and immutable.

The increase in urban land must also result in a continuing fall in the amount of land in agricultural use. In order to preserve the import saving potential of agriculture, the agricultural quality of land should continue to be taken into account in considering the precise location of urban development. However, the preservation of high grade agricultural land cannot be regarded as an overriding consideration and in each particular case the loss of agricultural production must be weighed against the benefits arising from development.

SCOPE FOR INFLUENCING POPULATION DISTRIBUTION

The future scope for policies designed to influence population distribution is governed by a wide variety of complex factors which the study analyses in some detail. Since any major planned expansion scheme represents a very considerable concentration of resources, decisions on a possible national strategy for population distribution should ideally be taken against a background of the relative costs and benefits, not only of alternative locations or alternative scales of growth but also of developing new large sites as against expanding existing major urban areas. But work on this subject so far has shown the complexities involved and progress is likely to be slow.

The rate at which any planned expansion scheme can be implemented is very largely dependent upon the availability of employment for the incoming population. Mobile industry is likely to remain in short supply for much of the 1970s and, outside the assisted areas, there seems little scope during this period for planned move-ment of a kind which would require mobile industry, beyond that already programmed or projected. These are, however, complex issues which need to be reviewed from time to time.

Finally the study has reviewed the role of the new and expanding towns in redistributing the population and considers the possi-bilities for further major developments of this kind. Since the war, about 800,000 people have been accommodated in new towns and town expansions and present plans provide for about a further 1 mil-lion to be so accommodated by 1981.

NEW MAJOR GROWTH AREAS

At a very early stage in the study, the very large increase in popu-lation by the end of the century then expected indicated a possible need for some major new population centres to accommodate part of this growth. Studies of selected areas—Humberside, Severnside and Tayside—which seemed *prima facie* suitable for such growth were therefore commissioned to ascertain the feasibility of large scale development in these areas. All three areas are, no doubt, physically capable of accommodating much larger populations than at present, but whether new developments on this scale will prove necessary or desirable, given the lower rate of population growth now expected and the practical constraints on population movement of this magnitude, is a question for further consideration and one which this study cannot attempt to answer.

IMPLICATIONS FOR FUTURE DEVELOPMENT

What then has the study demonstrated? Basically it was asked to examine the current population trends and, in the expectation of continued population growth, where the extra people would live. Long-term population forecasts have in the past undergone marked changes and may do so again; it is important therefore to remember their latent uncertainties. Continuous monitoring of population trends and their long-term planning implications is consequently essential. The questions of how the expected growth is likely to be distributed and whether any changes in the distributional pattern would be desirable, and feasible, raise some very complex issues. The study's examination of population movement in the past has shown that changes take place only relatively slowly and there are important social and economic constraints which effectively limit the scale on which movement can be induced. This suggests two possible and related conclusions. Firstly, that the broad regional distributional pattern of population at the end of the century may not be very strikingly different from what it is now. Secondly, that the greater part of the increase in population will probably be accommodated by the growth of existing centres and in overspill developments around the conurbations, with rather less emphasis on the development of major new areas of population and industrial growth at considerable distances from existing conurbations. This contrasts with the picture when the study was commissioned; considerable weight was then being given to the view that a significant redistribution of population might be necessary by developing one or more major new centres well away from the existing conurbations.

PROBLEMS OF THE MAJOR URBAN AREAS

This suggests that some of the most important planning problems of the next thirty years will arise in and around the existing conurbations and other major urban areas. As discussed earlier, population growth is by no means the only source of demand for new urban land. A considerable proportion of the housing in the conurbations and other large towns is either already obsolete or likely to become so by the end of the century. Although many of the people whose homes are redeveloped will be rehoused in the same (or nearby) areas, it is inevitable that considerable numbers of those displaced will need to be rehoused outside these congested areas, in part in new and expanded towns.

The conurbations, too, are also the areas where the greatest housing shortages are to be found and the alleviation of these shortages will add to the need for new housing land. Thus, population growth, population displaced by urban renewal, and present housing shortages all point to some of the most important problems arising in and around the existing major urban areas.

However, the full scale of the problems involved in accommodating the population up to the end of the century cannot be properly appreciated if the discussion is focused solely on the problems arising within the boundaries of existing large towns. It has been seen earlier how the pattern of urban settlement has been changing over the past forty years; how towns have, under the impact of successive improvements in communications, gradually extended to become more widely spread and less densely populated and to attract an increasing proportion of their work force from wider hinterlands. Also discussed was the way in which new towns, expanded towns and unsponsored movement have contributed to these natural tendencies. These twin forces have led to a situation where the fastest growing areas are those situated around the conurbations and all such areas now contain substantial populations. Thus, in considering where the main housing needs will arise in future, it is necessary to consider the conurbations and their surrounding areas as one, and on this basis it is clear that a significant proportion—certainly more than half—of the additional housing required will have to be provided in and around the city regions based on the major conurbations. There are also a number of other urban areas containing large populations not officially classified as conurbations and these too are likely to face similar housing problems, though on a relatively smaller scale.

Given the possible limitations on the promotion of long distance planned population movement, it seems likely that a considerable part of the additional housing needs of the conurbations will have to be met in some form of development located in their surrounding areas. The population pressures in such areas are likely to be severe. Not only will they be providing the main outlet for growth in the conurbations, but they themselves will also be experiencing rapid indigenous population growth. Moreover, the countryside in these areas is often of a special value as it provides the most readily accessible land for outdoor recreation for the inhabitants in the conurbations. These problems are of course not new. The advantages and disadvantages of large urban concentrations were considered in great detail in the report in 1940 of the Royal Commission on the Distribution of the Industrial Population (the Barlow Report). The Commission concluded that most of the disadvantages of large urban concentrations were not inherent in their size but rather resulted from the way their activities were organized, i.e. that basically they were unplanned. The Commission was not able to determine the point at which the disadvantages began to outweigh the advantages and hence did not reach any conclusion on the optimum size of settlements. Even so, the Commission were quite clear that whatever the ideal size of towns, London had long since exceeded it and recommended a check on London's growth and the dispersal of population and industry from congested areas. This major recommendation was accepted by the Government of the day and became a main feature of the distribution of population legislation introduced after the war.

CHANGES IN THE URBAN SETTLEMENT PATTERN

But while official encouragement has been given to planned dispersal from London and other conurbations to new towns and town development schemes created for the purpose, a great deal of unsponsored movement out of cities to their surrounding areas has also taken place. Such movement has not been accompanied to the same extent by a parallel movement of industry and although some migrants find work locally, many commute back to work in the main conurbations. Much of this unsponsored movement is to areas within about forty miles of the conurbations, roughly about the same distance as most of the planned expansion schemes. A situation has gradually come about where the population in the relatively densely populated inner areas of our towns and cities is falling, while rapid population growth is taking place beyond the green belts.

Thus, there has gradually emerged a new settlement pattern consisting of groups of towns standing in a hierarchial relationship to one or more major urban centres, the whole exhibiting a complex system of economic and social links. In many ways the activities carried out in this new settlement pattern correspond closely to those previously associated with cities, but unlike the city, the new urban pattern, often described as the city region, is characterized by a wide geographical spread of activities. This more widely dispersed pattern of development retains most of the general advantages associated with large populations, e.g. external economies for industry, ease of distribution of products, the provision of a wide variety of employment opportunities, a wide range of social facilities and amenities, while mitigating some of the disadvantages experienced with more densely populated urban areas. The nature of these areas demands that they should be planned as a whole.

In the shorter term up to about 1981, when taking account of new developments already planned and the likely limited supply of mobile industry, it seems inevitable that a considerable part of the housing need will have to continue to be met by further commuter developments within access of the main employment centres. The various economic and social interactions within city regions makes it desirable to ensure that the consequences and implications of the broad patterns of new development within the spheres of influence of the main conurbations are considered in the context of the needs and resources of the areas as a whole. Comprehensive plans for each conurbation and its surrounding area will therefore be needed to determine the desirable and efficient pattern of development.

STRATEGIES FOR FUTURE DEVELOPMENT

The recent changes in the planning system contained in the Town and Country Planning Act 1968 and the Town and Country Planning

(Scotland) Act 1969 will help to ensure that this is done. The new style structure plans will be concerned not only with the use of land but with the whole range of environmental and economic considerations which are vital to the proper planning of an area. But planning cannot be confined to the area of a single authority, however large; the circumstances of adjoining areas and even national considerations must be taken into account. A wider dimension is therefore needed in which these interests can be harmonized and which can form a framework for individual structure plans. Although the regional studies prepared by the Economic Planning Councils have fulfilled a useful function in identifying the main characteristics and problems of their areas, more definitive regional strategies will need to be developed. The ultimate aim should be to cover the whole country in this way, but the most pressing problems are likely to arise in and around the major conurbations. A major study of the South East has recently been completed by a joint team of central and local government planners and a similar study of the West Midlands, commissioned by the local planning authorities, is currently in progress, due for completion in 1971. In West Central Scotland, an area with half the population of Scotland, a strategy to co-ordinate the various proposals for the growth and redeployment of population is in course of preparation.

However, future land pressures are likely to be at their most acute in the North West region of England. Though the smallest of the English regions in area, it has by far the highest mean population density. There are serious problems of poor environment and extensive areas of outworn housing necessitating large scale programmes of urban renewal, with a considerable consequential redistribution of population. The problems of urban growth and redevelopment are rendered particularly complex by reason of the existence in this region of two conurbations, Merseyside and South East Lancashire with their centres only thirty miles apart. Although important land use/transportation studies have been mounted for each conurbation individually (the Merseyside study has been completed) their close physical proximity and the fact that they share to a considerable extent a common hinterland necessitates a broad strategic study of this area as a whole. The development of the Central Lancashire New Town, the problems of North East Lancashire which are the subject of separate study, and important proposals for Deeside, all add to the complexity of the planning problems of this region. A definitive regional strategy for the North West is thus urgently needed, since it is only in this wider context that the longer term implications of the complex physical and eco-

169

nomic inter-relationships of the two conurbations can be adequately assessed.

This study has tried to provide a broad background for planning the future population distribution of Great Britain over the next three decades. It is not, and cannot be, an authoritative guide to action. Many of the factors involved in this most complex of subjects are at present unquantifiable for more than a very few years ahead and, despite the very considerable advances in forecasting techniques, may remain so. As in all strategic planning, the main emphasis must therefore be upon flexibility. It is hoped that this study, tentative and provisional though its conclusions are, will provide a background for the examination of problems of population distribution, and a basis for further study and discussion.

Chapter 10

The Politics of Research—An Inaugural Lecture

J. B. CULLINGWORTH

In a true spirit of scientific inquiry, Mr Vice-Chancellor, I set about preparing for this inaugural lecture by looking up the dictionary definition of the verb 'to inaugurate'. I was only temporarily checked when I found that it was 'to make a public exhibition of for the first time'. I was rather startled, however, when, following up the lead 'see augur', I found that this was 'among the Romans, one who sought knowledge of secret or future things by observing the flight and the cries of birds'.

I felt that a little reflection might be more fruitful. This led me to the view that a professor with a new title would be expected not only to introduce himself to the academic community, but also to demonstrate that his subject was worthy of academic acclaim.

But what is my 'subject'? Urban and regional studies is a fine-sounding phrase but it can hardly be said to be unambiguous and precise. I thought it might be useful if I explored how other fields of study were defined. My exploration was an interesting one. I was surprised to find that long established 'subjects' had had agonizing introspections. History, geography, social psychology, anthropology and many others all seem to have had their doubters. And, judging by the earnestness with which their spokesmen discussed their essential identity they clearly had their sceptics.

I concluded that well-established fields of academic endeavour were familiar with the difficulties created by the unwritten conventions of academic trespass, and that these fields were not clearly circumscribed for ever by some intrinsic characteristic. I also concluded that any attempt to justify a new arrival would involve travelling over some well-worn ground. If I were not to become involved in questions which appeared to be at one point philosophical, at another semantic—but rarely substantive—my approach would have to be different.

But I also found—and my two years' experience as Director of the Centre for Urban and Regional Studies has amply confirmed this—that the problem-orientated, generalist academic has problems other than those of demarcation, particularly when he comes, as I do, from another non-discipline like social administration. As Professor Titmuss has put it:

> Generalists, and those who conceive their subject as having an integrative function in teaching and research, are confronted with a particular occupational hazard in attempting to give reasons for their existence. In the eyes of others, they may seem to be saying 'Why then, the world's mine oyster.'[1]

In my interpretation 'Urban and Regional Studies' has close affinities to social administration (and it is no accident that it has a particular attraction to social administrators). Neither is an academic discipline in the conventional sense in which this term is used. Neither has a distinctive corpus of knowledge or a specific theoretical structure. Both, indeed, are academic mavericks.

Professor Donnison, in his Inaugural Lecture at the London School of Economics, spoke of social administration as being concerned with 'an ill-defined but recognisable territory: the development of collective action for the advancement of social welfare'.[2] Students of social administration seek 'to identify and clarify problems within this territory, to throw light upon them—drawing light from any discipline that appears to be relevant—and to contribute ... to the solution of these problems'.

In precisely the same way Urban and Regional Studies focuses on the 'problems' of urban areas and their regions. It is impossible to draw meaningful boundaries to this field of study. It is also unprofitable. The issues which are 'relevant' are too many and too diverse. The disciplines to be employed range over the whole of the social sciences and beyond; and they cannot be limited in advance. Any science or art—from mathematics to aesthetics, from cybernetics to sociology, from engineering to history—may have significant contributions to make to a fuller understanding of particular urban and regional issues.

This is not to make preposterous claims for a new *Programme of Scientific Work Required for the Re-organization of Society* in the manner of Comte.[3] On the contrary the objectives are modest: to bring the skills of a variety of academics from a range of disciplines to bear on a number of selected urban and regional issues.

But all this amounts to a non-definition. Indeed, the more I tried to devise a meaningful definition, the more I appreciated my unconscious wisdom in not having tried before. And since there is no claim for an academically defensible 'discipline' the selection of issues for study rests on pragmatic considerations.[4]

172

It was at this point that I felt that rather than inaugurate my field of study, I might attempt to augur—to conjecture from signs and omens—on the organization of social research. Since one of the matters I wished to discuss was the impact of contracts and 'terms of reference' on university research, it seemed appropriate that I should not be too closely bound by precedent and the unwritten conventions which may apply to an Inaugural Lecture. (In passing I might comment that I was glad to find that there was no convention —as there is for a new Member of Parliament—that my maiden speech should deal only with non-controversial matters.)

I wish, therefore, to spend much of my time discussing an issue which appears to me to be of crucial significance not only for the development of social science, and the relationship between social science and public policy, but also for the future role of universities. Nevertheless, I must say something about the nature of urban and regional studies as I see it, not only because this is expected of me, but because my views on this have a direct bearing on the main issues I want to bring before you tonight.

As I see it the role of urban and regional research is to increase our understanding of social and economic forces in order that policies can be developed to secure an improvement in economic functioning and in the quality of the social and physical environment.

If we are to understand the functioning of cities and regions we must first be able to answer a number of apparently simple questions about who lives where and why; about the location of jobs; about the forces—economic, social and governmental—which affect these; about styles of life and aspirations; and about the linkages between all these things—in terms, for example, of communications, mobility and change.

Yet, in spite of the fact that that each year, nearly a tenth of the population move, we know remarkably little about who moves where and why. We are able to describe and map certain patterns of growth and decline, but our understanding of the dynamics of change is extremely limited. Furthermore, we are very much slaves to the statistics which are available to us. We have, for instance, an extraordinary abundance of figures on persons and rooms and can thus measure the intensity of use of housing space to several decimal places. But the flow of these statistics has increased at the very time when they are of increasing irrelevance. They have utility in demonstrating that issues such as 'under-occupation in subsidized council houses' are in reality 'non-issues'. What we do not know is the significance of the intensity of use of housing space in the dynamics

173

of urban change. Indeed, we do not know how far housing conditions as measured by our traditional indices are as important as conditions on which we do not have indices—the quality of the physical environment, the standard of public and social service for instance. It could be that a crucial factor lies even further afield—in the relationship between the cost of labour and the cost of materials. Vernon has suggested that this is a factor of some importance:

> in a nation whose economy places a heavy price on hand labour and a low price on materials, the cost of repairs and remodelling can easily outrun the cost of new construction. Like economic men, therefore, the children of the middle class have moved to the modernity of the split-level-in-the-suburbs, leaving many of the older middle-income neighbourhoods to stagnate or decline.[5]

The American situation is not, of course, necessarily relevant in Britain either now or in the future, though its prolific commentators render us an invaluable service in constantly suggesting new lines of inquiry which can be followed—or ignored—with profit.

For instance the incredible spread of American cities is made possible (and accelerated) not only by the far greater role played by personal transport and the sheer abundance of land, but also by the outward movement of jobs. In the United States about half of the urban labour force serves the local population and follows a population move (in this country the proportion is lower, but is on the increase). More significantly, much American manufacturing industry has joined the outward move.

In Britain suburban growth has been largely residential: the jobs have remained—and increased—in the urban areas. An important influence here (though I hesitate to guess how important) has undoubtedly been the planning controls which have operated in a framework which denied that suburban residential development would take place. The objective of this policy has been to restrain 'urban sprawl' and to provide for growth and 'overspill' in 'self-contained communities' beyond the green belt where people could both live and work. This classical concept has proved impracticable: housing pressures have been irresistible, but the controls over industrial development (operated within a wider context of regional policy and by a government department different from that responsible for housing) have apparently been much more effective. To the extent that they have been effective, however, the British suburbanite has been denied the range of job opportunities open to his American counterpart.

Recent evidence suggests that the outward movement of population has gathered momentum and that jobs in the towns are on the decline. This may be the beginning of the emergence of an American-type pattern. We cannot say at the present, though it is crucially important that we attempt to find out. In the meantime, the dynamics of change in British cities look different from those in the United States. Here, a major problem for working class families moving out to suburban locations is that of the journey to work of the chief wage earner and the shortage of local jobs for secondary earners (particularly women with young children) who *cannot* commute. There are thus suburban housing opportunities but limited job opportunities.

The American situation is the obverse of this. The poor are trapped in the low-income housing market but their jobs are moving out.[6]

A significant element in the difference stems, of course, from the role played by local authority housing in Britain. It is this which has enabled large numbers of working class families to move to suburban locations. At the same time local authorities have undertaken very extensive redevelopment. The impact of this major intervention in the housing market demands much greater attention than it has yet received. Unfortunately, attention has focused on political issues such as the equity of housing subsidies and rent controls, rather than on the effect of these devices and their institutional framework on urban change.

In a similar manner, the public sector itself has focused its attention on a limited aspect of the urban complex: that of the physical fabric. The British programme of slum clearance and redevelopment (which has no equal anywhere in the world) has brought about a remarkable physical change. But little attention has been paid to the impact of this on the social and economic structure and functioning of the city.

The redevelopment of an area involves a change not only in its physical characteristics, but also in its social and economic character and function. One obvious change—in the British context—is that the people who live in a redeveloped area will be those who are 'eligible' for council houses. This eligibility has to be defined in a way which is defensible in political terms: houses are allocated on the basis of need as defined by publicly accountable politicians and as interpreted by administrators. This is quite different—conceptually at least—from the market and social situation which exists in the private sector. There, demand and supply, rents and ability to pay, and acceptability to property owners and managers determine who shall live in the area. How different are the results of these two systems? Are the two markets quite different?—or, if other terms are preferred, do the two systems cater for different categories of need?

Little by way of an answer can be given, though it is clear that, overall, certain categories of need are increasing both as a result of the change brought about by public action and as a result of wider social and economic forces. For instance, increases in mobility, in the ability of the young single person to maintain a separate household, and in the number of students are general trends leading to a rise in the demand for non-family type accommodation. At the same time there is a shrinking supply of bed-sitters and lodgings.

Equally important is the effect of redevelopment in reducing the supply of cheap accommodation. Redevelopment involves not only the clearance of poor quality housing: it also decreases the cheap housing market. Higher building costs, higher enforced housing standards, and pressures to adopt 'realistic' rent policies may all conspire to price council housing out of the range of poorer families. And, unattractive as this may be to social reformers (whether of the academic or political type), some families prefer low housing costs to high housing standards.

This complex of issues is—to my mind—the very stuff of Urban and Regional Studies. The term 'complex' is apposite, since they are all inter-related. The abstraction of one part of the complex, whether by the single-discipline academic or the single-minded politician, constitutes a journey into the unreal.

In the sphere of physical planning this understanding has come to the fore and has led to a rejection of the concept of a twenty-year development plan and its replacement by flexible strategies. Unfortunately, our understanding of the forces which planners seek to control is so inadequate that there is a danger of flexibility becoming expediency—the very negation of planning.

The essential ingredient of planning is prediction. Urban and regional studies, if they are to be anything more than cross-disciplinary intellectual gymnastics, are similarly concerned with prediction. If prediction is impossible, urban and regional studies must be largely an academic extravagance—stimulating and absorbing, maybe, but little else. Prediction, however, demands an understanding of the present and an identification of the relevant determinants. It is easy to show how wrong past predictions have been in many fields: population, car ownership and use, the demand for electricity, doctors and higher education, to name but a few.

But these projections are typically concerned with one factor only. Others may be taken into account but only as subservient blocks of data to enable the variable at issue to be computerized. Indeed, extremely important inter-related variables may be omitted completely. For example, in predicting future levels of car ownership and use in British cities one must take into account the future form of these cities and the distribution of economic activities and housing developments within them. It is as inadequate to ignore these in projecting car ownership and use as it is to predict future urban form without having regard to the motor car.[7]

Webber has argued that 'extrapolations of past trends are no longer reasonable, if only because extrapolation implies that past determinants of trend lines will persist into the future', and that 'projections of qualitative change must precede quantitative forecasts'.[8]

There is a fallacy here—which could lead us into the field of science-fiction utopianism (particularly if we are led along by Webber's lyricism into accepting that 'to a considerable degree, maybe we really can invent the future').

The inadequacy of extrapolations is that they have traditionally dealt with results rather than causes—the number of births rather than the determinants of attitudes to family size; the number of individuals participating in a recreational activity rather than the motivations of recreationalists; the number of cars rather than the reasons why people buy and use cars.

In short, they have been based on an inadequate understanding of the present. Pressures to predict—particularly from government—have led to premature projections.

The increasing concern of government with prediction and planning has had a considerable impact on the politics of social research. Despite the disdain with which policy makers and administrators have traditionally regarded 'research' there is now an increasing awareness of its usefulness. This carries its own dangers. Flattering though it might be to the social scientist to be regarded as a magician who can plumb the depths of the unknown, the truth of the matter is that his technical competence extends over a very limited field. The researcher can speak with authority only within this limited field (which may not even be the most relevant to the issue in question), but it is likely that he will be asked to pronounce (and feel inclined to pronounce) on related or contextual issues well beyond his technical competence. Being a human being as well as a scientist he may well fall into the trap: indeed his social conscience may make him feel compelled to do so.

As Price has put it:

At some point in the process of studying and deciding on any social problem the boundaries of expert knowledge end, and the realm of responsible judgement begins. But all too often the scientist fails to recognize that he has gone beyond the boundaries of what can be proved by research and is speaking *ex cathedra* on matters on which his own judgement is just as personal, and perhaps nearly as prejudiced, as any layman's.[9]

Quite apart from the validity of the social scientist's views outside his own field of expertise, this excursion into the world of politics may throw doubts on the validity of his judgement in the field where he is competent.

The persistent academic clamour for 'pure' research is in part a defence-mechanism against this: academic integrity is easier to safeguard if relationships with public affairs are studiously avoided.[10]

But what is the character of this 'purity' about which we hear so much? There has for long been a debate in the physical sciences on the distinctions between various types of 'pure' and 'applied' research. There appears to be general agreement that a categorization is useful, though, as the Zuckerman Report pointed out, 'there is and can be no clear-cut line of demarcation between one form of research and another; basic research and development are, so to speak, bands at opposite ends of a continuous spectrum'. Furthermore, 'most organizations engaged in research will be concerned to some extent with the whole range of research and development'.[11] Ben-David has argued that 'there is no reason why some applied research should not be also fundamental research and vice versa. If a piece of research—whatever its original aim—results in publication which is a contribution to knowledge and also leads to the solution of a practical problem, then it is both'.[12] Pierre Auger has suggested that the distinctions can no longer be drawn by reference to the research objective or even to the methods employed. Instead, 'the best criterion might perhaps be the lasting motive which impels the research worker to continue his work in each individual case'.[13]

Thus, if a piece of research comes to an end when an immediate practical problem is solved it is 'applied', but if the researcher goes on to explore the field he has penetrated it is 'pure'. Presumably the same can be achieved if a 'pure man' takes over where an 'applied man' leaves off. Be that as it may, one is constantly struck by the truth of Lancelot Hogben's statement that 'science thrives by its applications'.[14]

The crucial element in all research is that of defining questions in researchable terms. Research design involves reformulating broad issues into relatively simple questions amenable to inquiry. The greater is the simplification (or abstraction) the purer is the research operation. The scientific paradigm is Physics:

In Physics, when we find a complicated object that cannot be described in simple goemetry or by a few equations, we knock it into smaller pieces, or we purify and recrystallize it, or we cool it down, or we heat it up, until it becomes amenable to mathematical analysis.[15]

Such a reduction to the 'mathematically amenable' is, however, the exception rather than the rule, though it may remain the goal to which researchers in both the physical and the social sciences aspire —in spite of the fact that it dates from a bygone era of scientific certainty, before the revolutions of quantum theory and relativity.[16] In practice all research is essentially 'intuitive, uncertain, deeply felt and controversial':[17] and the same situation applies whether one is examining the properties of high energy cosmic ray particles,[18] or the demand for owner-occupation in the new towns. Few fields of research can lead to pure, incontrovertible conclusions. The search for purity, for the mathematical, is certainly premature (to put the matter no more strongly) in the social sciences. Indeed, too great a concentration of effort on the seemingly pure may lead to an exaltation of method over matter.

It is, however, quite wrong to assume that the distinctions between 'pure' and 'applied' in the physical sciences are relevant to the social sciences. The Heyworth Committee seemed to accept some distinction, but did not make clear what the distinction was.[19] I share Professor Simey's view that no case has been made: 'in what sense is "basic" work basic, and "applied" research applied?'[20] The distinction is meaningless. The Heyworth Committee in reality underlined this when they stated that 'the social and human factors which affect the application of research are themselves a part of the subject of the research'.

Part of the problem is that the fundamental propositions of social science:

seem so obvious as to be boring, and an intellectual, by definition a wit and a man of the world, will go to any mad lengths to avoid the obvious. Add to this the dilemma created by the assumption that making fundamental discoveries is the mark of science. Then either, if its fundamental propositions are already well known and so need not be discovered, social science cannot be a science, or, if it is a science, its principles must remain to be discovered and so must be other than these.[21]

Social science is inherently 'applied': it is the application of objective methods of inquiry to the functioning of society.

If I may digress for one moment:
One of the major inadequacies in social research has been its lack of concern for the *use* of research. It is extremely wasteful to invest large resources in research activity if the results are underutilized (or even rejected), simply because appropriate resources have not been invested in research on the nature and operation of the human institutions which must interpret and use research.[22] In the physical sciences, the British inadequacy in developing the discoveries of penicillin and radar are classical examples. In the social sciences the signs are encouraging—and, to social scientists, flattering—but it could be that major advances in social science will be jeopardized by the lack of intellectual investment in crucial areas (including that of the use of social research), a concentration of activity in a heady rush towards a premature and inappropriate mathematical accuracy, and a preoccupation with theoretical models emanating from intellectual inventiveness rather than from attempts to provide an orderly frame for the facts of social and economic life.

The categorization of research into 'pure' and 'applied' would simply be a piece of intellectual fun—rather like devising clear definitions which distinguish between the various social sciences— if it were not for the important implications which are thought to follow for the organization of research, for the role of universities and the role of government. A simple minded view holds that pure research should be carried out in universities and that applied research is the business of government. If this were true, the results would be disastrous for universities and for government. There are some suggestions that this could happen and thus the issue is one of important practical significance.

The signs are to be found in the acclaim which has followed the recommendations of recent reports for an expansion of research within the framework of government. Of course, no contemporary committee of inquiry can fail to conclude that an expansion of social science research is required—whether it be for local government (Herbert, Seebohm and Maud) or central government (Fulton), but there has been little discussion of the organization of research within the machinery of government, its relationship with research in universities and the impact of 'government research' on universities as institutions of research and education.

Here I can only pose some of the issues. The starting point is the character of higher education, the essential feature of which is membership (even if only temporary) of the scientific community. The hall-mark of this is the spirit of inquiry, the unceasing challenging of fact, theory, assumption, belief and dogma. (Universities, like all human institutions, do not always live up to their ideals, but that is another matter.)

The character of higher education is thus essentially the same as the character of scientific research. 'Higher education and fundamental research are therefore logically part of a single co-ordinated endeavour the aim of which is the creation and diffusion of new knowledge, first and foremost to a specialized scientific community and those apprenticing themselves to this community and only secondly to an undefined general public.'[23]

But universities do not exist in isolation, and their relationship with the wider society is more than a matter of social responsibility: it is of crucial significance to their ability to maintain their scientific character. If universities fail to meet the needs of the wider society, other institutions must develop separately from them. It is here that I am apprehensive of the development of major research institutions outside universities.

The attraction of non-university research organizations must not, however, be minimized. On the contrary, these attractions need to be analysed since they reflect on the current inadequacies of universities and indicate the lines along which university reorganization is required. First and foremost is the inadequate support provided in universities for research. In the words of the OECD Report on the Ministerial Meeting on Science:

While the university provides in general the best surroundings for creative fundamental research, its circumstances are often far from ideal. Universities have their origin in the public need for higher education, and while lip-service is paid to research, it is often included as an after-thought. Many university teachers of great research ability are overloaded with teaching and routine administration and are not able to give to their research the concentration and sustained attention which really pioneering investigations require. Research budgets are often provided separately by governments, thus encouraging the universities to provide for teaching as a matter of course, but for research only on a modest scale. Some universities may be too narrow in their traditions to encourage outstanding research schools which initially appear to be unconventional. In Europe, more than in the United States, compartmentalization on the basis of obsolete divisions of learning makes it difficult to initiate either study or research in new fields, especially if these are uncomfortably astride rigid departmental barriers.[24]

This was written with reference to the physical sciences and in relation to Western Europe as a whole, but the points strike some familiar chords in relation to the social sciences in British universities. I would add: the intense pressure on British universities to expand their student intake; the widespread belief in some academic circles that social research is a privileged activity; and—more pernicious— the belief that research staff are essentially apprentices who, when they have completed their research, will graduate to a teaching position. Inferior status, lack of tenure, and even lower salary scales are common indications of this.

In such circumstances it is not surprising that research posts in a non-university organization devoted to research have a particular attraction for the would-be social researcher. If the philosophy of the recent report of the Prices and Incomes Board [25] were to be accepted this attraction would undoubtedly increase.

None of this is intended as an argument against research being undertaken in independent research institutes or within the machinery of government. My concern is that the inadequate organization and support for research in universities could lead to a major hiving off of an important university function which could have serious consequences for universities, for the development of social science, and for the real contribution which social science can make to social policy.

The problem facing research work within the machinery of government is essentially that it easily becomes the handmaiden of policy. Yet, as the Fulton Report has pointed out it is important for government that research should 'not become too much detached from the main stream of the department's work'.[26] But how far can research worthy of the name be undertaken unless it is detached? On the other hand, what impact on policy is detached research likely to have?

I can only pose the questions and suggest that some part of the answers could be found by looking at the experience of the Home Office Research Unit, the Ministry of Housing Research and Development Group (particularly its sociological research section), the Civil Service Pay Research Unit, the Greater London Council's

Research and Intelligence Unit, and similar units which have been set up in recent years.

What is the quality of research which such organizations carry out? Can they attract and retain staff of high calibre? I find it significant that the Zuckerman Committee found it necessary to discuss whether government research establishments should undertake basic research in order to 'help recruitment and provide an intellectual stimulus for the staff'.[27]

I maintain, however, that the Zuckerman categorization of research activities is invalid for the social sciences, at least at their present stage of development. The crucial issue in the social sciences is who is to set the questions: the research worker or the sponsor. Put in this way, the issue is as relevant to research carried out in universities but supported by government funds as it is to research carried out within the machinery of government. The freedom of the social researcher—and hence the scientific nature of his work— is largely illusory if he is entirely constrained by terms of reference laid down by a public authority (whatever its degree of enlightenment) and by deadlines set by a financial time-table.

Research undertaken within a university can—and must, question questions. It must ask not simply whether a given policy is adequately designed to meet its objectives, but how these objectives relate to social and economic forces, and how they relate to other policy objectives. Above all, it must seek a better understanding of the social and economic issues with which policy is concerned.

These questions should be raised within the machinery of government, but given that all institutions have a built-in resistance to change, it is unlikely that they will be, at least on the scale and with the intensity required. 'Change in goals and functions is difficult to bring about without external criticism',[28] and what better base for criticism is there than the scientific community of a university?

Indeed, one must go further. Ben-David's review of *Scientific Productivity and Academic Organization in Nineteenth Century Medicine* [29] shows that the growth of scientific discoveries was due to increased opportunities for entering research careers. 'Continuous growth represents a situation in which research becomes a regular career; fluctuations, a situation in which research to a large extent is a spontaneous activity engaged in by people as the spirit moves them.' Ben-David concludes that his review suggests that 'the growth of discoveries in any field may be limited by the capacity for expansion of the institutional framework'.

It must not be forgotten, however, that the subject matter of the social scientist is also that of the politician. It is not without good reason that the term 'academic' has a very specific connotation outside the walls of the university. If social research is to make a contribution to social welfare it has to develop techniques of communication and influence. Unfortunately, despite the social scientist's preoccupation with human behaviour, he has not exhibited any remarkable proficiency in the practice of the skills which he studies. In part this is due to his traditional political insensitivity, his isolation from the responsibility for policy and, perhaps above all, his preoccupation with a small part of the whole—strengthened by the organization of universities on the lines of individual 'disciplines'.

The great advantage of social research undertaken by or sponsored by government is that it brings research workers into close contact with an operating system as distinct from an abstracted aspect of a problem. A closer relationship between government and universities can be of benefit to both social science and the practice of government. But a balance has to be preserved: and it is not an easy one to achieve. Professor Cherns has highlighted the problems in a paper summarizing his impressions of a visit to social science research organizations in Israel, India, Australia and the U.S.A.[30] He points out that it is in the universities where one sees 'at their purest, the social forces which inhibit the utilization of research'. Research workers and administrators operate within quite different time-scales: by the time a research project is complete the original problem facing the administrator and which precipitated the support for a study will have changed (and the administrator is likely to have changed as well). Even more important, the objectives of the university and the administration are different:

> Universities are not really organized so as to make interdisciplinary research easy, nor will the young scientist risk working in interdisciplinary areas if his career prospects are thereby endangered— as they are. Thus, the research worker in the universities will approach a problem from the basis of his own discipline, and for him the effective problem is that part of the total problem which is accessible to his analytical framework and dissectible by his analytical tools. This may not even be recognizable to the administrator as the problem which confronts him; nor will the solution, if one is offered, be likely to be one he can accept, as it will not take into account all the pressures to which he is subjected.

What then of non-university research organizations? These are of two kinds: those within the machinery of government and those which are, nominally at least, 'independent'. The former tend to fall into two categories, according to which pit has ensnared them.

The first, which is the most common, is the one where the Director of Research has identified himself with the employing organization, 'accepting the values and priorities of the administrators':

> The natural history of the research division presided over by the Director who has 'sold out' to the administrator is a common exhibit in the zoo of academic disasters. He, the Director, starts with aspirations of a programme which will contrive a balance of long-term, medium and short-term projects. He will sadly tell you that, as time has gone on, he has become more and more concerned with studies of immediate and short-term relevance and that he had had to put aside the longer-term studies. He may even make a virtue out of this and contrast the speed of his operation with the dilatoriness of his friends in the universities. At the worst, he will actually block, if he can, any approach from his organization to a university or vice versa. He will also tell you how difficult it is to get and retain good research workers; how the good ones have gone off to academic appointments, leaving him with those whom he did not particularly wish to keep.

> The natural history of the division presided over by the other kind of Director is different, but equally painful. Here the Research Director looks to the academic community and the publications in scientific journals for his rewards. To preserve his academic freedom and scientific objectivity, this Director has effectively insulated himself and isolated himself from the administration. Not only have the administrators lost interest in the research he is doing, but they may even go elsewhere—to their friends in universities for example—to get a quick answer to a factual question rather than endure a mystery being made of a simple query. There are less serious problems in this division of obtaining and retaining good research workers, but from the point of view of the organization as a whole they might as well be on the other side of the moon. In either case, utilization of research, other than of simple fact-gathering, is at a discount.

The independent research institute receives less comment in Professor Cherns' paper, but after noting its freedom from the pressures of an administration and from the constraints imposed by the teaching function of a university, he pinpoints the problem which derives from the constant need to secure financial support.[31]

> This reaches the extreme position in the U.S.A. where, owing to the need for project directors to raise the money for their own salary—as well as for the salaries of the other members of the

team—they not only spend a good deal of their time in administration, but also have too little opportunity to participate in the kind of cross-fertilization between projects that the research institute offers as one of the justifications for its existence.

So we see difficulties in any organization of social research. Many of these difficulties can, I think, be overcome by a far greater interchange of staff, for example, between different types of research units and between research units and administrative bodies. But given current institutional frameworks this is not feasible on any significant scale. A review of these frameworks and their interrelationships with the structure of universities and the structure of government is overdue. It would be a tragedy if this issue were lost in a preoccupation with a search for new forms of local government and a new pattern of local-central government relationships. In my view the organization of research cannot be divorced from the wider problem of devising 'a political system by which the freedom of research can be defended and its results applied to practical problems under the guidance of responsible democratic processes'.[32]

I must now try to summarize. A better understanding and a closer relationship is needed between researchers and policy-makers. This is required both for the development of social science and for the contribution which social science can make to policy. The issue becomes of increasing importance as government funds for research increase. British universities, like their American counterparts, are likely to be compelled to follow the young lady from Kent:

> There was a young lady of Kent
> Who said that she knew what it meant
> When men took her to dine
> Gave her cocktails and wine
> She knew what it meant—but she went.

It is no answer to suggest that research funds must be sought from men having no ulterior motives. 'Cocktails and wine' have the same attraction and effect irrespective of who provides them. Independent sources of finance are very important, but they cannot absolve universities from their responsibilities.

Science cannot exist on the basis of a treaty of strict non-aggression with the rest of society. . . . Our argument for the freedom of science must rest on the conviction that such freedom is justified both by the importance of freedom for its own sake, as the fundamental value in political society, and by the historical evidence that only free science can play a dynamic role in furthering human welfare.[33]

But social scientists must take care that their commitment does not lead them astray. Social researchers tend, by their nature to be socially conscious: their interest in social problems tempts them to jump too quickly from description to prescription. They are too ready 'to expect macrosocial problems to submit themselves to mere social scientific manipulation or to think that the policy advice of social scientists is magically efficacious'. This is a 'denial of the statesman's art and a burdening of the social scientist with what he is incompetent to handle'.[34]

A flight into the esoteric, into premature grand model-making, into the supposedly value-free atmosphere of 'pure' social science, is no answer to this problem. A social scientist may or may not be reluctant to take on responsibility for policy guidance, but he cannot contract out of the society which is the subject of his study.[35]

Yet, as the notorious Project Camelot demonstrated, social science and public policy must be separated in significant ways. Social science must maintain its autonomy: without it 'the very concept is severely jeopardized', and 'the corruption of social science on a scale hitherto unimagined' is possible. The larger problem here is not the submerging of scientific inquiry into contract fulfilments, nor 'the feasibility of social science, but the credibility of social scientists'.[36]

In their preoccupation with meeting the needs of society for an increased supply of highly-educated manpower, and their own problems of internal communication and the organization of power, universities may ignore an equally important issue of their relationship with the wider society.[37] Project Camelot and Moynihan Report [38] demonstrate clearly that this issue is of crucial significance not only in the context of the function of universities but also in that of the 'politics of controversy'.

The purpose of research is 'to bring political controversy closer to realities'.[39] It must seek to understand, but not to asssume the political perspective of policy-makers. The organization of research must therefore be independent—but not remote—from the arena of action.

Careful note must be taken of the implications which follow from the increasing role of research in the formulation of public policy. I am sure that Price is correct when he suggests that:

the development of public policy and of the methods of its administration owes less in the long run to the processes of conflict among political parties and social or economic pressure groups than to the more objective processes of research and discussion among professional groups.[40]

It is my belief that the higher purposes of government, of social science, and of universities are best served by a major freely committed research element within universities. Though much research of value to all three can—and inevitably must—be undertaken outside universities, large shifts of effort in this direction, however justified in the short term, may have disastrous long-term consequences. Two years' experience of directing a university research department have made me less sure that my ideal is realizable, but this still remains my article of faith.

References

1. R. M. Titmuss, 'The Subject of Social Administration', in *Commitment to Welfare*, Allen & Unwin, p. 13.

2. D. V. Donnison, 'The Development of Social Administration' in *Social Policy and Administration*, by D. V. Donnison, V. Chapman and others, Allen & Unwin, 1965, p. 26.

3. The title of August Comte's famous prospectus embodying his comprehensive social philosophy.

4. See *The Work of the Centre*, University of Birmingham Centre for Urban and Regional Studies, Occasional Paper No. 4, 1969.

5. R. Vernon, *The Myth and Reality of our Urban Problems*, Harvard University Press, 1962, p. 35.

6. To quote Vernon again:

'out-commuting—the movement each morning of people from homes in the center portions of the urban area to jobs on the periphery—is growing fast. The spectacle of groups of blue-collar workers, travelling outward by car pool against the flow of incoming traffic, is now a common sight on the roads of many large cities. In fact, the spotty and fragmentary information on this phenomenon suggests that it may be one of the fastest-growing streams of traffic among the complex currents of our urban areas.' Op. cit., pp. 44–45.

7. M. E. Beesley and J. F. Kain, 'Urban Form, Car Ownership and Public Policy: An Appraisal of *Traffic in Towns*', *Urban Studies*, Vol. 1, No. 2, November 1964, pp. 174–203.

8. M. Webber, 'Planning in an Environment of Change', *Town Planning Review*, Vol. 39, No. 3, October 1968, p. 193.

9. D. K. Price, *Government and Science*, New York University Press, 1954, p. 133.

10. In Merton's words, 'the exaltation of pure science is thus seen to be a defence against the invasion of norms which limit directions of potential advance and threaten the stability and continuance of scientific research as a valued social activity'. R. K. Merton, 'Science and the Social Order', in *Social Theory and Social Structure*, Free Press, revised edition 1957, p. 543.

11. *The Management and Control of Research and Development*, HMSO, 1961, p. 7.

In Zuckerman's categorization, *pure basic research* is concerned simply with scientific knowledge. Significantly, 'a line of "pure basic" research is selected by the individual worker to satisfy his own tastes and intellectual curiosity'.

Objective basic research is undertaken in fields of recognized potential technological importance: it is characteristically stimulated primarily by technological needs.

Applied research has a definite practical goal. Where this goal is a new process or piece of equipment, Zuckerman terms it *project research*. Applied research aimed at improving the use of an existing process or piece of equipment is *operational research*.

Finally, *development* is the bridge between research and production. It is defined as 'the work necessary to take, for example, a new process or piece of equipment to the production stage'.

12. Joseph Ben-David, *Fundamental Research and the Universities*, OECD, 1968, p. 17.

13. Pierre Auger, *Current Trends in Scientific Research*, UNESCO, 1961, p. 17. To continue the quotation:

'Pasteur, for instance, somewhat reluctantly agreed, on the advice of J. B. Dumas, to take up the study of a silkworm disease—pebrine. He embarked on it with a practical aim and, being a chemist and not a biologist, he did not apply the principles of the 'disinterested' biology of his day, but the logical principles more akin to those of chemistry. As soon as a method of combating the disease was discovered, the 'applied' research, the research with an essentially practical object, should have come to an end and the scientist should have turned to other studies. But Pasteur was a truly disinterested scientist; he wanted to understand; he wanted to know. It was this new motive which led him, after his research on milk, wine and beer, to open a completely new chapter in biology. Needless to say, his pursuit of pure knowledge has had very important practical implications.'

14. L. Hogben, *Science for the Citizen*, Allen & Unwin, 1957, p. 741. The passage in which this occurs is worth quoting in full:

'To get the fullest opportunities for doing the kind of work which is worthwhile to themselves, scientific workers must participate in their responsibilities as citizens. Among other things, this includes refraining from the arrogant pretence that their own preferences are a sufficient justification for the support which they need. This pretence, put forward as the plea that science should be encouraged for its own sake, is a survival of Platonism and of the city-state tradition of slave ownership. Science thrives by its applications. To justify it as an end in itself is a policy of defeat.'

15. J. Ziman, *Public Knowledge: The Social Dimension of Science*, Cambridge University Press, 1968, p. 41.

16. See Werner Heisenberg, *Philosophic Problems of Nuclear Science*, Faber, 1952. Simey (to whom I am indebted for the reference) writes:

'Much confusion has been occasioned by the fact that many social scientists seek to adopt the model of Victorian physics as their prototype of science, oblivious of the scientific revolutions of the early twentieth century which established a new mode of science, armed with new concepts and new aspirations, and exchanged the scientific uncertainty of today for the dogmatism of the nineteenth century. The claims of 'science' to an understanding of universal truth, eternally valid in the objective facts of nature, are much more hesitant and much more qualified that they were a century ago . . . the concept of science, if it is to be applied to social as well as physical phenomena, must be very substantially adapted and developed for the purpose . . . this will require very substantial modifications in our thinking. The result may be to bring the work of physical scientists much nearer that of social scientists, an outcome that it will be generally agreed, is very much to be desired.' (T. S. Simey, *Social Science and Social Purpose*, Constable, 1968, pp. 23–24.)

17. J. Ziman, op. cit., p. 72.

18. The example given in the Zuckerman Report of 'pure basic research' (p. 7).

19. *Report of the Committee on Social Studies*, Cmnd. 2660, HMSO, 1965: 'As in all fields of study basic and applied research are both essential if knowledge is to advance; and it would be an error to imagine that in the social sciences work proceeds in isolation and can be applied only when it has advanced far enough. Basic research and applied research have to be carried out simultaneously; neither can advance without the other.' (para. 89).

20. T. S. Simey, op. cit., pp. 179–181.

21. G. C. Homans, *The Nature of Social Science*, Harcourt, Brace and World, 1967, p. 73. (Cf. E. Devons, 'Applied Economics—The Application of What?', in *Essays in Economics*, Allen & Unwin, 1961.)

22. 'There is no direct relationship between specific kinds of fundamental research and the eventual applications of the findings in practice . . . success in exploiting science for practical purposes does not, therefore, result from the guidance of fundamental research by practical considerations but from constant entrepreneurial activity aimed at bringing to the attention of potential users whatever may be relevant for them in science and vice versa'. (J. Ben-David, *Fundamental Research and the Universities*, OECD, 1968, p. 56.) Related problems are the ability of the machinery of government to pose research questions and to interpret research findings. Research requires intelligent consumers as well as intelligent producers!

23. J. Ben-David, op. cit., p. 18.

24. Op. cit., pp. 28–29. See also Ministerial Meeting on Science: *Fundamental Research and the Policies of Governments*, OECD, 1966, p. 55.

'Since research in some of the areas of natural science is so expensive, it has proved easier, and it is probably wiser, to provide funds for the totality of university needs for instruction and to supplement the contributions for research in the sciences by separate mechanisms. To provide such funds through general grants to universities is seldom satisfactory. Most universities have their origin in a public demand for education and, correspondingly, they tend to budget for instruction as a matter of course and provide for research when there is something over. Since pressure for higher education always increases more rapidly than the available funds, research financed from general university budgets tends to be neglected although such funds as are forthcoming represent the freest resource for research.'

25. National Board for Prices and Incomes, *Standing Reference on the Pay of University Teachers in Great Britain: First Report*, HMSO, Cmnd. 3866, 1968.

26. *The Civil Service: Vol. 1: Report of the Committee*, Cmnd. 3638, p. 57.

27. They rejected this proposal, and argued that 'pure basic research' is best carried out in universities and that, 'if the promise of such work ever became an overt inducement to recruitment' in government establishments, it might 'lead only too often to so-called fundamental work being pursued in a backwater remote from the main stream of scientific activity and with little concern for practical applications, and that in the long run it would neither help recruitment nor provide an effective intellectual stimulus'. (*The Management and Control of Research and Development*, HMSO, 1961, p. 28.)

28. R. M. Titmuss, 'The Health and Welfare Complex' in *Commitment to Welfare*, Allen & Unwin, p. 75.

29. *American Sociological Review*, Vol. 25, 1960, pp. 828–843; reprinted in B. Barber and W. Hirsch, *The Sociology of Science*, Free Press, 1962. (The questions are from p. 327).

30. A. Cherns, 'The Art of the Useful—2', *Social Science Research Council Newsletter*, No. 3, May 1968, p. 29.

31. Independent research institutes face the problems of a chronic shortage of finance, isolation from the main stream of scientific activity, and a separation of research and teaching. On the other hand they can have a freedom of action which is rare in universities and they are not subject to the problems of disciplinary boundaries. (See, for example, *Research in Political Science*, Social Science Research Council, Reviews of Current Research No. 1. Heinemann, 1968, p. 11).

In the physical sciences some concern has been expressed at the 'ageing' of independent research institutes. 'Indeed, in some government institutions . . . a staff of almost uniform age grows old together and the throughput of young scientists can be very small.' The university provides a striking contrast: 'Combination of the unorthodox and intuitive probing of young scientists with the experience and judgement of the more mature research worker takes place spontaneously in the university research environment and greatly favours the maintenance in them of a high degree of originality.'

A non-university institute has to take steps to safeguard standards. Though they can—and do—carry out brilliant work 'it is more difficult for such institutions to retain high standards of creative work over long periods'. (*Ministerial Meeting on Science*, op. cit., pp. 30–31.)

I would expect that such problems are not likely to be significant in the social sciences. The very nature of social science and its close relationship with policy would tend to bring about a mobility between research and administration thus creating space for a constant flow of younger research workers. Nevertheless, the issue needs to be watched.

32. D. K. Price, op. cit., p. 107.

33. D. K. Price, op. cit., pp. 106–107.

34. K. H. Silvert, 'American Academic Ethics and Social Research Abroad: The Lesson of Project Camelot', in I. L. Horowitz (ed.), *The Rise and Fall of Project Camelot*, M.I.T. Press, 1967, p. 93.

35. See R. Boguslaw, 'Ethics and the Social Scientist', in I. L. Horowitz, op. cit., p. 118:

'Values play an important role implicitly (though characteristically not explicitly) in the formulation of research projects. The selection of 'safe' areas for investigation specifically introduces a biasing factor into the range of scientifically established alternatives available to policy makers. It introduces a similar bias into the character of scientific information and analysed situations available in the chronicles of social science. This is a responsibility and a risk which every scientist must take every time he formulates, conducts, or interprets the results of his studies.'

36. I. L. Horowitz, 'Social Science and Public Policy: Implications of Modern Research', in I. L. Horowitz, op. cit., pp. 339–376.

37. A contrary view has been expressed by President Stratton of the Massachusetts Institute of Technology. Concerned at the impact on the Universities of the sheer bulk of scientific research, he argues:

'There is a basic incompatibility between the true spirit of a university and those elements of management which tend to creep into the organization of projects, the planning of programmes, and the utilization of costly facilities. One must ask whether the universities can by themselves satisfy the need for all the fundamental research that appears necessary in this country and whether it is wise for them to attempt to do so . . . One must recognize that there may be an ultimate need to establish central institutions to supplement the universities in fundamental research. . . . If we strive to contain the widening scope of research entirely within our large universities, we shall end by changing their character and purpose. In so doing, we shall render the greatest possible disservice to the cause of research itself.'

(J. A. Stratton, 'Research and the University', *Chemical and Engineering News*, Vol. 31, No. 2582, June 22, 1953, quoted by C. V. Kidd in B. Barber and W. Hirsch, *The Sociology of Science*, Free Press, 1968, p. 408.)

This, however, relates to the massive impact of Federal research programmes in the physical sciences. The situation in relation to the social sciences is fundamentally different, at least in the forseeable future.

38. On Project Camelot see I. L. Horowitz, op. cit.; on the Moynihan Report, see L. Rainwater and W. L. Yancey, *The Moynihan Report and the Politics of Controversy*, M.I.T. Press, 1967. See also D. P. Moynihan, *Maximum Feasible Misunderstanding*, Free Press, 1969.

39. The phrase is from C. Wright Mills, *The Sociological Imagination*, Oxford University Press, N.Y., 1959, p. 64.

40. D. K. Price, op. cit. Cf. M. Webber, 'Planning in an Environment of Change', *Town Planning Review*, Vol. 39, No. 3, October, 1968, p. 184: 'The knowledge industry is fast becoming the new centre of influence and power, with the universities and the "R. & D." firm assuming the roles that corporations and labour unions have recently occupied.' See Chapter 1 of this volume, p. 30.

Index